OECD DOCUMENTS OCDE

THE DISTRIBUTIVE EFFECTS OF ECONOMIC INSTRUMENTS FOR ENVIRONMENTAL POLICY

◆

EFFETS DISTRIBUTIFS DES INSTRUMENTS ÉCONOMIQUES DANS LA POLITIQUE DE L'ENVIRONNEMENT

PUBLISHER'S NOTE

The following texts have been left in their original form to permit faster distribution at lower cost.

NOTE DE L'ÉDITEUR

Les textes reproduits ci-après ont été laissés dans leur forme originale pour permettre
pour un coût moindre, une diffusion plus rapide.

ORGANISATION FOR ECONOMIC CO-OPERATION AND DEVELOPMENT
ORGANISATION DE COOPÉRATION ET DE DÉVELOPPEMENT ÉCONOMIQUES

ORGANISATION FOR ECONOMIC CO-OPERATION AND DEVELOPMENT

ORGANISATION DE COOPÉRATION ET DE DÉVELOPPEMENT ÉCONOMIQUES

Pursuant to Article 1 of the Convention signed in Paris on 14th December 1960, and which came into force on 30th September 1961, the Organisation for Economic Co-operation and Development (OECD) shall promote policies designed:

— to achieve the highest sustainable economic growth and employment and a rising standard of living in Member countries, while maintaining financial stability, and thus to contribute to the development of the world economy;

— to contribute to sound economic expansion in Member as well as non-member countries in the process of economic development; and

— to contribute to the expansion of world trade on a multilateral, non-discriminatory basis in accordance with international obligations.

The original Member countries of the OECD are Austria, Belgium, Canada, Denmark, France, Germany, Greece, Iceland, Ireland, Italy, Luxembourg, the Netherlands, Norway, Portugal, Spain, Sweden, Switzerland, Turkey, the United Kingdom and the United States. The following countries became Members subsequently through accession at the dates indicated hereafter: Japan (28th April 1964), Finland (28th January 1969), Australia (7th June 1971) and New Zealand (29th May 1973). The Commission of the European Communities takes part in the work of the OECD (Article 13 of the OECD Convention).

En vertu de l'article 1er de la Convention signée le 14 décembre 1960, à Paris, et entrée en vigueur le 30 septembre 1961, l'Organisation de Coopération et de Développement Économiques (OCDE) a pour objectif de promouvoir des politiques visant :

— à réaliser la plus forte expansion de l'économie et de l'emploi et une progression du niveau de vie dans les pays Membres, tout en maintenant la stabilité financière, et à contribuer ainsi au développement de l'économie mondiale ;

— à contribuer à une saine expansion économique dans les pays Membres, ainsi que les pays non membres, en voie de développement économique ;

— à contribuer à l'expansion du commerce mondial sur une base multilatérale et non discriminatoire conformément aux obligations internationales.

Les pays Membres originaires de l'OCDE sont : l'Allemagne, l'Autriche, la Belgique, le Canada, le Danemark, l'Espagne, les États-Unis, la France, la Grèce, l'Irlande, l'Islande, l'Italie, le Luxembourg, la Norvège, les Pays-Bas, le Portugal, le Royaume-Uni, la Suède, la Suisse et la Turquie. Les pays suivants sont ultérieurement devenus Membres par adhésion aux dates indiquées ci-après : le Japon (28 avril 1964), la Finlande (28 janvier 1969), l'Australie (7 juin 1971) et la Nouvelle-Zélande (29 mai 1973). La Commission des Communautés européennes participe aux travaux de l'OCDE (article 13 de la Convention de l'OCDE).

Applications for permission to reproduce or translate all or part of this publication should be made to:
Les demandes de reproduction ou de traduction totales ou partielles de cette publication doivent être adressées à :

M. le Chef du Service des Publications, OCDE
Head of Publications Service, OECD
2, rue André-Pascal, 75775 Paris cedex 16, France

FOREWORD

The OECD is carrying out a series of projects on the use of economic instruments in environmental policy. One project consisted of an assessment of the possible distributive consequences of these instruments. This work was carried out under the supervision of the OECD Group on Economic and Environment Policy Integration. The present report has been prepared by Dr. David Harrison Jr., Vice President of National Economic Research Associates (Cambridge, Massachusetts, USA). It is published under the responsibility of the Secretary-General. It is available in the English language only (a summary in French is included).

Dr. Harrison gratefully acknowledges partial support from the Economic Department and the Public Management Service of the Organisation for Economic Co-operation and Development (OECD) as well as from a grant by the United States Environmental Protection Agency. Helpful comments were also provided by participants in two OECD workshops and by members of the OECD Group on Economic and Environmental Policy Integration.

AVANT-PROPOS

L'OCDE a entrepris une série de projets relatifs à l'utilisation des instruments économiques dans les politiques de l'environnement. L'un de ces projets a consisté à évaluer les éventuels effets distributifs de ces instruments. Ces travaux ont été menés sous la supervision du Groupe de l'OCDE sur l'intégration des politiques économiques et de l'environnement. Le présent rapport, établi par M. David Harrison Jr., Vice-Président de National Economic Research Associates (Cambridge, Massachusetts, Etats-Unis), disponible en anglais seulement (accompagné d'un résumé en français) est publié sous la responsabilité du Secrétaire général.

M. Harrison est particulièrement reconnaissant au Départment des affaires économiques et au Service de la gestion public de l'Organisation de coopération et de développement économiques (OCDE) du concours qu'ils lui ont apporté, ainsi qu'à l'Agence pour la protection de l'environnement des Etats-Unis pour la subvention dont le projet a bénéficié. Les participants à deux réunions de travail de l' OCDE et les membres du Groupe de l'OCDE sur l'intégration des politiques économiques et de l'environnement lui ont également fourni de précieux commentaires.

ALSO AVAILABLE

Climate Change, Designing a Practical Tax System (1992)

Climate Change, Designing a Tradeable Permit System (1992)

Taxation and Environment (complementary policies 1993)

TABLE OF CONTENTS

LIST OF FIGURES

LIST OF TABLES

EFFETS DISTRIBUTIFS LIES A L'UTILISATION D'INSTRUMENTS ECONOMIQUES DANS LES POLITIQUES DE L'ENVIRONNEMENT

RESUMÉ ET CONCLUSIONS

Dans le monde entier, les pressions exercées sur les pouvoirs publics afin qu'ils trouvent des solutions aux problèmes d'environnement se font de plus en plus fortes; ce faisant, ils sont confrontés à la nécessité de parvenir à faire s'entendre des groupes dont les avis sont très différents. Cette divergence de vues tient en partie au fait que tout choix politique n'a forcément pas les mêmes répercussions sur les différents groupes. Un phénomène de résistance est probable de la part des groupes qui sont perdants, ou qui estiment qu'ils risquent d'être lésés. Il peut s'ensuivre une paralysie, ou une situation médiocre.

Les enjeux environnementaux sont de plus en plus importants. Le réchauffement global, la diminution de la diversité biologique, l'appauvrissement de la couche d'ozone, la prolifération des substances toxiques, les pluies acides, le smog dans les villes, la disparition des zones humides sont autant de problèmes d'environnement appelant des solutions parfois très coûteuses. Selon certaines estimations, le coût des mesures proposées pour la réduction des émissions de gaz à effet de serre représente de un à trois pour cent du produit intérieur brut d'un pays. Ce coût et d'autres s'ajouteraient aux sommes consacrées à la protection de l'environnement, qui, dans de nombreux pays de l'OCDE, sont actuellement comprises entre un et deux pour cent du produit intérieur brut. Ces coûts risquent d'augmenter, et les conséquences distributives de ces politiques vont s'avérer d'une importance croissante.

I. LES INSTRUMENTS ÉCONOMIQUES EN TANT QUE MOYENS DE RESOUDRE LES PROBLEMES D'ENVIRONNEMENT

Les instruments économiques suscitent un intérêt croissant de la part des responsables politiques et de ceux qui sont chargés d'élaborer les règlements, car ils offrent la promesse d'un allégement des coûts et d'une plus grande souplesse dans la réalisation des objectifs en matière de protection de l'environnement. En janvier 1991, le Conseil de l'Organisation de Coopération et de Développement économiques a adopté une Recommandation par laquelle il est recommandé aux pays Membres de "faire un usage plus fréquent et plus cohérent des instruments économiques ..." (OCDE 1991a, p.3). Cette Recommandation est le reflet de l'augmentation du nombre de cas dans lesquels il est fait appel à des instruments économiques, et où il est proposé des politiques allant dans ce sens.

Parmi les exemples les plus significatifs, on peut citer la proposition formulée dans de nombreuses instances internationales, relative à l'instauration d'une taxe mondiale sur le carbone et d'un système de permis négociables pour les émissions de carbone, le système de taxe sur le carbone que certains pays européens, notamment en Scandinavie, se proposent d'instituer ou qu'ils appliquent d'ores et déjà, ainsi que le programme de permis négociables pour les émissions de substances provoquant des pluies acides, récemment adopté aux Etats-Unis.

A.   Concept de base

Le système des instruments économiques repose sur un concept fort simple. (Le présent résumé ne traite que des taxes et des permis négociables ; pour une analyse de l'ensemble des instruments économiques déjà employés ou susceptibles de l'être à des fins de protection de l'environnement, on se reportera aux publications OCDE 1989 et 1991c). Les pouvoirs publics définissent les objectifs généraux à atteindre en matière de protection de l'environnement, comme par exemple le niveau des émissions de gaz à effet de serre, mais ils laissent les forces du marché déterminer quels sont, du point de vue des coûts, les moyens les plus efficaces pour atteindre ces objectifs. Du fait de cette liberté laissée aux forces du marché, les réductions d'émissions interviennent là où la diminution coûte le moins, si bien que, globalement, le coût de la lutte antipollution est moins élevé qu'avec un système classique basé sur une réglementation contraignante. Sur le long terme, le prix résultant de l'application d'une taxe ou d'un système de permis négociables incite également davantage à trouver de nouveaux moyens (moins onéreux) de lutte antipollution. En résultat net, la lutte antipollution coûte globalement moins cher. (Les argument théoriques plaidant en faveur du recours aux incitations économiques ont été développés dans de nombreuses études, cf. notamment Ackerman et Steward (1988), Anderson et al. (1977), Dales (1968), Hahn et Hester (1989), Kneese et Schultze (1976), Nichols (1984), OCDE (1991b), Pearce, Markandya et Barbier (1989), Schelling (1983), Stavins (1988), ainsi que Tietenberg (1985)).

La perspective de voir le coût global de la lutte antipollution diminuer ne suffit cependant pas à garantir le dégagement d'un accord quant à l'adoption d'une taxe ou d'un programme de permis négociables. Comme toute mesure politique, l'application d'instruments économiques peut être bloquée en raison de l'opposition de ceux qui estiment qu'ils risquent d'être lésés. En fait, comme les instruments économiques constituent une nouveauté, les obstacles auxquels on se heurte lorsque l'on veut les appliquer sont encore plus grands que ceux qui sont à surmonter lorsque l'on veut recourir à une stratégie traditionnelle impliquant une réglementation contraignante, stratégie dont la plupart des pays de l'OCDE sont, au bout de plusieurs décennies, parvenus à peaufiner les aspects fondamentaux.

Il ressort de ces considérations que les partisans des instruments économiques doivent en étudier les effets *distributifs*. Jusqu'à présent, il en a été très peu tenu compte. Deux questions se posent :

1.   En cas de recours à des instruments économiques, qui sont les gagnants, et qui sont les perdants ?

2.   Quelles sont, le cas échéant, les mesures susceptibles d'atténuer les éventuels effets négatifs ?

En tentant d'apporter une réponse à ces questions, les responsables de l'action publique peuvent appréhender à quel point il est difficile de parvenir à un accord lorsque le débat politique porte sur des enjeux extrêmement sensibles.

B.   Objectif du présent projet

Cette étude avait pour principal objectif la définition d'un cadre systématique pour l'évaluation des effets distributifs. Ce document ne donne pas de recommandation sur l'opportunité d'utiliser ou non les instruments économiques, en complément ou en substitut à d'autres instruments. On part du principe selon lequel *il faut impérativement* déterminer qui sont les gagnants et qui sont les perdants, *avant même* de négocier et de conclure un accord portant sur l'utilisation ou la non-utilisation des instruments économiques et sur les programmes correspondants.

L'élaboration d'un cadre pour l'analyse des effets distributifs comporte un certain nombre d'étapes qui correspondent approximativement aux sections du présent document. La première étape consiste à traiter les problèmes "de seuil" qui se posent avant de passer au stade de l'analyse proprement dite et de la collecte des données. Au cours de la deuxième étape, on élabore un cadre conceptuel pour l'analyse. La troisième étape consiste à résumer les données empiriques existantes (relativement succinctes) en matière d'effets distributifs. L'évaluation des mesures pouvant être prises afin d'atténuer les effets négatifs fait l'objet de la quatrième étape. A partir des indications obtenues au cours de ces quatre étapes successives, on peut dresser une liste récapitulative des principaux problèmes, et dégager un certain nombre de conclusions, lesquelles sont reproduites *in fine*.

II. QUESTIONS À RÉGLER AVANT D'ENTREPRENDRE UNE ANALYSE DES EFFETS DISTRIBUTIFS

Avant d'entamer une étude systématique des problèmes d'ordre distributif, il est essentiel de définir la *nature* de l'analyse à effectuer. Même si quelques uns de ces problèmes se posent également dans le cas d'une analyse d'efficience, ils ont davantage d'acuité lorsqu'il s'agit des effets distributifs dans la mesure où les options offertes sont beaucoup plus nombreuses et où le consensus est moindre quant au champ que doit recouvrir l'analyse.

1.   Par rapport à quelle situation de référence faut-il mesurer les effets distributifs ?

De toutes les questions à régler d'entrée de jeu, celle-ci est peut-être la plus importante. On peut envisager deux cas diamétralement opposés : (1) soit on effectue une analyse dans l'absolu, en partant de l'hypothèse selon laquelle il n'existe *aucune* réglementation en matière d'environnement ; (2) soit on procède à une analyse comparative en prenant comme référence une situation se caractérisant par l'application d'une réglementation contraignante censée produire des résultats équivalents. Par exemple, on pourrait comparer les effets du système de permis négociables mis en place aux Etats-Unis pour les émissions à l'origine de pluies acides à ceux obtenus soit *en l'absence de tout* contrôle fédéral sur les émissions de ce type provenant des centrales en exploitation, soit dans l'hypothèse d'une réglementation contraignante visant à réduire dans les mêmes proportions les émissions provenant des centrales. .

Dans la plupart des cas, il semble qu'une analyse *comparative* permette de mieux mettre en évidence l'impact relatif des instruments économiques qu'une analyse dans l'absolu des avantages liés à l'application de tel ou tel instrument en particulier. Cette démarche est du reste celle qui est suivie lorsqu'il s'agit de juger de l'efficience d'ensemble ; on évalue les économies réalisées du point de vue des coûts en faisant la *comparaison* avec les coûts encourus dans le cas d'une réglementation classique.

Le fait d'opter en faveur de la méthode comparative a trois conséquences. Premièrement, il faut définir une alternative réglementaire *unique* pouvant servir de base de comparaison pour l'évaluation des effets distributifs. Deuxièmement, il n'est généralement pas tenu compte, dans les analyses comparatives, des *avantages* retirés du point de vue de l'amélioration de l'environnement. (Ces avantages peuvent d'ailleurs évoluer si les émissions varient dans le temps où géographiquement à la suite de la mise en place d'un système de permis négociables ; cf. dans Nichols et Harrison 1990b l'étude d'un cas concret dans lequel le passage à un système de permis négociables s'est traduit par une diminution de la pollution atmosphérique). Troisièmement, comme les instruments économiques permettent de réduire le coût global de la lutte antipollution, le problème n'est plus de déterminer la répartition des coûts, mais celle des *économies* réalisées.

Dans certains cas toutefois, il est plus logique d'évaluer les effets distributifs en prenant comme base de référence une situation de "non-réglementation". L'exemple qui vient immédiatement à l'esprit est celui de la taxe sur le carbone ; les nombreuses analyses effectuées à ce propos consistent davantage à évaluer les effets de cette taxe en tant que telle qu'à les comparer à ceux qui seraient obtenus si, pour réduire les émissions de carbone dans les mêmes proportions, on empruntait la voie réglementaire. De plus, dans certains cas, il sera souhaitable d'évaluer des politiques qui <u>combinent</u> les instruments économiques et la réglementation. Pour déterminer la situation de référence, il importe de considérer quelles politiques seraient adoptées, le cas échéant, en l'absence d'instruments économiques.

2. Les instruments économiques doivent-ils être générateurs de recettes publiques ?

Les taxes sur les émissions et les systèmes de permis négociables présentent généralement une grande similitude, tant du point de vue de leur efficience que pour ce qui est de leurs effets distributifs. Il existe toutefois une différence essentielle suivant que les instruments économiques sont ou non générateurs de recettes publiques. Il importe ici de faire une distinction entre deux types d'instruments économiques, à savoir (1) les taxes et les permis mis en vente, qui sont dans les deux cas sources de recettes publiques, et (2) les permis fondés sur les droits acquis, attribués "gratuitement" aux entreprises, et qui ne sont donc pas une source de recettes publiques.

3. Faut-il évaluer à la fois les incidences *initiales* et les incidences *finales* ?

Initialement, les instrument économiques ont pour première incidence de faire augmenter les recettes publique et d'accroître (ou de diminuer) le coût de la lutte antipollution. Les avantages pour l'environnement sont probablement importants eux aussi si l'on prend comme base de comparaison une situation de non-réglementation. Une grande partie du débat a trait aux incidences initiales, tant il est vrai que les entreprises s'inquiètent des répercussions que l'application d'instruments économiques peut avoir sur leurs coûts. Ainsi, comme nous le notons ci-dessous, les petites entreprises de Los Angeles craignent d'être les plus touchées par le système de permis négociables en cours d'élaboration.

Toutefois, il est également intéressant d'avoir une idée de la charge que ces effets représenteront *en fin de compte* ; qui, en définitive, sera lésé et qui sera avantagé ? L'analyse des incidences finales doit être effectuée en tenant compte de deux principes (Musgrave et Musgrave, 1984). Premièrement, c'est toujours au niveau des *individus*, qu'il s'agisse d'actionnaires, de contribuables, de consommateurs, ou de salariés, que les coûts et les bénéfices se situent en fin de compte. Deuxièmement, lors de l'évaluation des charges assumées et des avantages retirés en tout dernier ressort, il faut tenir compte du fait qu'il existe de nombreux moyens de transférer d'un groupe à un autre les coûts et les avantages. L'exemple le plus probant est celui des hausses de prix, par lesquelles les entreprises s'efforcent de transférer les coûts des actionnaires aux consommateurs.

4.   Faut-il mesurer à la fois les effets transitoires et les effets à long terme ?

La répartition dans le temps des effets à analyser pose un problème du même ordre. Si l'on met l'accent sur les incidences finales, cela signifie que l'analyse doit porter essentiellement sur les effets à long terme. Tout comme les analyses relatives à l'incidence de l'impôt, les analyses consacrées aux effets distributifs consistent généralement en une évaluation des impacts, après ajustement à un nouvel équilibre des prix et des quantités. Dans ce genre d'analyse, on fait abstraction des augmentations de coûts intervenant pendant la *phase de transition* - c'est-à-dire pendant la période au cours de laquelle s'opèrent les ajustements entre un régime réglementaire et un autre (Baumol et Oates, 1988, Harrison, 1978).

L'effet transitoire le plus visible est le chômage provoqué par la diminution de la production. Dans les analyses statiques comparatives de type classique, portant sur le long terme, on ne tient pas compte de ces effets transitoires ; on part du principe que les ressources en main-d'oeuvre ou en capital sont utilisées dans d'autres secteurs de l'économie. Ces effets transitoires occupent cependant une place de tout premier plan dans les débats publics suscités par les changements de politique, aussi bien sur le plan national qu'international.

Les effets transitoires doivent-ils être pris en compte ? Même si d'aucuns prétendent qu'on leur accorde une importance excessive -- les salariés pouvant être exagérément pessimistes quant à la durée de la période pendant laquelle ils risquent d'être au chômage -- il semble important de préciser clairement les emplois et les entreprises susceptibles d'être touchés, ainsi que les mesures qui pourraient, le cas échéant, être prises afin de limiter les pertes.

5.   Sur quels groupes doit porter l'analyse des effets distributifs ?

En général, dans les analyses économiques portant sur les effets distributifs, on s'attache essentiellement à examiner les répercussions pour les différentes *tranches de revenus*. Comme pour les impôts, on s'efforce de déterminer si les coûts sont régressifs (plus lourds à supporter pour les couches les plus démunies) ou progressifs (plus lourds pour les hauts revenus).

En fait, de nombreux autres regroupements en catégories peuvent s'avérer intéressants. Nous avons déjà signalé qu'il pouvait être utile d'étudier différents types d'entreprises (petites entreprises par rapport aux grandes entreprises, ou différentes branches industrielles), ainsi que les salariés considérés en tant que groupe. Des regroupements géographiques (à l'intérieur d'un pays ou entre plusieurs pays) et par classes d'âge pourraient également être intéressants.

6.   Quelle technique de modélisation convient-il d'employer ?

La série d'effets susceptibles d'être évalués est fonction de la technique de modélisation employée. Il existe une multitude de possibilités à cet égard, allant des simples calculs informels à l'élaboration de modèles compliqués d'équilibre général, simulant le fonctionnement de systèmes économiques nationaux (ou internationaux) tout entiers. La plupart des analyses consacrées aux effets distributifs reposent cependant sur une approche relativement simple, celle de l'équilibre partiel. Un tel modèle est valable lorsqu'il s'agit d'analyser les effets d'une politique dont l'impact est essentiellement ressenti au niveau d'un segment relativement étroit de l'économie. Pour les politiques plus complexes, ou ayant une plus grande portée -- cas notamment d'une taxe nationale sur le carbone -- il est nécessaire d'avoir une approche plus globalisante.

III. APERCU THEORIQUE

Les principes traditionnels de la micro- économie offrent un cadre théorique pour l'estimation des effets que l'application d'instruments économiques peut initialement avoir sur les coûts des entreprises et de l'incidence finale de ces variations de coûts sur les différents groupes de consommateurs. On peut se servir d'un cadre théorique similaire pour apprécier les avantages que les différents groupes peuvent en retirer du point de vue de l'environnement. Depuis de nombreuses années, l'évaluation de l'incidence des politiques fiscales et, dans une moindre mesure, des avantages de divers programmes se fait par référence à ces principes. Cependant, avant d'exposer ces principes d'analyse, nous présentons un cadre, établi en tenant compte des différents points évoqués jusqu'à présent, qui clarifie les principaux éléments à prendre en considération.

A.   Cadre pour l'analyse des effets distributifs

Il ressort de l'examen des questions à régler au préalable qu'il n'existe pas de formule *unique* pour analyser les effets distributifs. A la figure 1 sont énumérés les éléments qui entrent en ligne de compte selon les réponses apportées aux trois questions-clés suivantes :

1. Par rapport à quelle situation de *référence* les effets sont-ils évalués ?

2. Les instruments économiques sont-ils ou non générateurs de *recettes publiques* ?

3. Les effets sont-ils à long-terme *ou* ont-ils un caractère transitoire ?

Les mentions de la quatrième colonne correspondent à un ensemble de choix effectués à l'aide de ce cadre. (Ces choix ont été en partie inspirés par une taxinomie développée par le Dr. Stephen Smith, à qui nous adressons nos plus vifs remerciements pour sa contribution). Elles donnent une idée des résultats que l'on peut espérer obtenir, par rapport à une situation de référence caractérisée par une réglementation contraignante produisant les mêmes résultats, quant à la qualité de l'environnement, avec un système de permis négociables attribués non pas par voie d'enchères, mais en fonction des droits acquis (cas applicable aux effets du système de permis négociables récemment mis en place aux Etats-Unis pour les émissions de substances responsables des pluies acides). Les coûts pour les entreprises diminuent parce que le coût de la lutte antipollution est moins élevé et que le système n'est pas générateur de recettes publiques. Dans une perspective à long terme, l'analyse ne révèle aucune autre incidence initiale (sauf peut-être au niveau des coûts administratifs assumés par les pouvoirs publics). Il faudrait peut-être, lors de l'analyse des effets transitoires, étudier l'impact potentiel pour les industries (charbon à haute teneur en soufre, par exemple) et pour les salariés (pour les mineurs par exemple). Les points d'interrogation signifient que l'on ne sait pas exactement si les coûts transitoires sont plus ou moins élevés avec des instruments économiques que dans un régime de réglementation contraignante.

Le principal enseignement que l'on puisse retirer de cette taxinomie est peut être que, lorsque l'on veut apprécier les effets distributifs d'un programme fondé sur des instruments économiques, la première chose à faire est de cerner clairement les enjeux. L'analyse peut être différente selon les hypothèses retenues à propos des trois choix à faire. Nous nous appuierons sur les données de ce tableau lorsque nous étudierons le cadre théorique proposé pour évaluer les effets distributifs correspondant aux principales catégories d'incidences initiales, à commencer par celles sur les coûts des entreprises.

B.   Analyse des effets à long terme

L'analyse des effets distributifs à long terme commence par une évaluation des incidences initiales. La figure 1 donne une liste des incidences par rapport à deux situations de référence différentes, à savoir une situation de non réglementation et une situation caractérisée par une réglementation contraignante. (Pour un examen plus détaillé des points soulevés dans cette section, se reporter à Nichols et Harrison, 1991, ainsi qu'à Harrison et Nichols, 1992).

1.   *Situation de référence caractérisée par l'absence de réglementation*

Si l'on prend comme référence une situation de non-réglementation, la mise en oeuvre d'un système de taxes ou de permis négociables se traduit initialement par une augmentation du coût de la lutte antipollution pour les entreprises et les ménages, par une augmentation des frais administratifs que la puissance publique doit supporter pour faire fonctionner le système et par des avantages accrus du point de vue de l'environnement. Les taxes et les permis d'émission attribués par voie d'enchères sont également générateurs de recettes publiques.

La détermination de l'incidence finale est la plus directe dans le cas des coûts et des avantages initiaux pour les ménages. Par exemple, un train de mesures destiné à réduire les émissions des véhicules à moteur peut faire augmenter les coûts d'utilisation des véhicules, mais conduire à une amélioration de la qualité de l'air dans différentes régions. Pour déterminer la répartition de ces coûts suivant les tranches de revenus, on peut s'appuyer sur les informations disponibles quant au budget automobile des ménages en fonction du groupe de revenus dans lequel ils se situent. Pour déterminer la répartition des avantages par tranches de revenus, on peut s'appuyer sur les informations disponibles quant à la structure des revenus dans les régions où la qualité de l'air s'est améliorée (cf. Harrison et Rubinfeld, 1978b). Sur la base d'études visant à estimer la valeur en dollars que les ménages accordent à l'amélioration de la qualité de l'air, on peut attribuer une valeur en dollars aux changements concrètement intervenus dans ce domaine. Il est alors possible d'apprécier l'effet net (coûts moins avantages) des mesures pour les différentes tranches des revenus.

La détermination des ménages qui, en fin de compte, assument les coûts initialement supportés par les entreprises nécessite des analyses supplémentaires. Compte tenu de l'importance accordée à la lutte contre la pollution d'origine industrielle, les coûts supportés par les entreprises représentent dans la plupart des cas l'essentiel des dépenses engendrées par les programmes de lutte contre la pollution ; même le coût de la lutte contre la pollution automobile est essentiellement assumé au départ par les constructeurs et par les compagnies pétrolières. Sur le plan théorique, ces analyses sont simples et reprennent le schéma suivi pour analyser l'incidence des taxes sur les produits. Comme dans ce dernier cas, le coût de la lutte antipollution est à la charge soit des consommateurs, qui doivent payer des prix plus élevés, soit des actionnaires, qui voient baisser les bénéfices des sociétés. La ventilation des coûts entre les deux groupes dépend de l'élasticité relative de l'offre et de la demande; lorsque la demande est relativement peu élastique (auquel cas les entreprises parviennent à transférer les coûts vers les consommateurs), ce sont les

Figure 1. Incidences initiales des instruments économiques

Incidence initiale	Situation de référence			
	Pas de réglementation directe		Réglementation contraignante	
	Taxes/Permis d'émission attribués en fonction des droits acquis (1)	Permis d'émission attribués par voie d'enchères (2)	Taxes/Permis d'émission attribués en fonction des droits acquis (3)	Permis d'émission attribués par voie d'enchères (4)
Analyse des effets à long terme				
Entreprises				
Coûts de la lutte anti-pollution	Augmentation	Augmentation	Diminution	Diminution
Taxe/Achats de permis d'émission	Augmentation	Aucun effet	Augmentation	Aucun effet
Gouvernement				
Recettes fiscales/Vente de permis d'émission	Augmentation	Aucun effet	Augmentation	Aucun effet
Coûts administratifs	Augmentation	Augmentation	Diminution (?)	Diminution (?)
Ménages				
Avantages du point de vue de l'environnement	Augmentation	Augmentation	Aucun effet	Aucun effet
Coûts de la lutte antipollution	Augmentation	Augmentation	Diminution	Diminution
Analyse des effets transitoires				
Coûts pour les entreprises	Augmentation	Augmentation	Augmentation (?)	Augmentation (?)
Pertes d'emplois	Augmentation	Augmentation	Augmentation (?)	Augmentation (?)

consommateurs qui assument l'essentiel de la charge ; lorsque la demande est relativement élastique (auquel cas les consommateurs peuvent résister aux tentatives visant à leur transférer les coûts), ce sont les actionnaires qui en supportent la majeure partie. L'analyse des effets que l'attribution de permis d'émission en fonction des droits acquis peut avoir sur les prix présente une difficulté d'ordre théorique. Bien que, pour les entreprises, les permis fondés sur les droits acquis, qu'elles ont obtenus "gratuitement" afin de couvrir leurs émissions, n'entraînent aucune charge financière supplémentaire, l'utilisation de ces permis pour couvrir les émissions résiduelles fait intervenir un "coût d'opportunité", qui se répercute sur la fonction de coûts de l'entreprise et en fin de compte sur le prix des produits. En résultat net, on aura des prix plus élevés, reflétant à la fois le coût des ressources supplémentaires mobilisées afin de réduire les émissions et le coût d'opportunité lié à l'utilisation des permis pour couvrir les émissions qui subsistent malgré les mesures de lutte contre la pollution.

L'étape suivante consiste à traduire les augmentations de prix appliquées par les industries fabriquant des biens intermédiaires ou fournissant des matières premières en hausses au niveau du prix des produits finis et des services. Une fois ces hausses évaluées, on analyse les effets distributifs de la même manière que pour les coûts initialement supportés par les particuliers. On peut, pour apprécier la charge qui incombe en fin de compte aux consommateurs appartenant aux différentes tranches de revenus, utiliser les informations disponibles sur les dépenses que les ménages consacrent aux différents types de produits suivant la tranche de revenus dans laquelle ils se situent. Ensuite, on peut déterminer la charge qui incombe en fin de compte aux actionnaires appartenant aux différentes tranches de revenus à partir des informations disponibles sur l'actionnariat dans chacune de ces tranches.

2. *Situation de référence caractérisée par une réglementation contraignante*

Lorsque la situation choisie comme référence se caractérise par une réglementation contraignante, la démarche de fond est la même. Il convient de déterminer l'ampleur des incidences initiales pour les entreprises, pour la puissance publique et pour les ménages, puis d'évaluer les incidences finales pour les différents groupes classés par niveaux de revenus ou selon d'autres critères. A certains égards, cette analyse *comparative* est plus facile à réaliser que lorsque l'on prend comme référence une situation de non-réglementation mais, sous d'autres aspects, elle se révèle plus difficile :

-- dans les études comparatives, il *n'est pas nécessaire* d'analyser la répartition des avantages retirés du point de vue de l'environnement ; en revanche,

-- il est *indispensable* d'évaluer les économies que, grâce aux instruments économiques, les entreprises et les ménages réalisent sur les coûts de la lutte antipollution.

La principale *raison d'être* du recours à des instruments économiques pour lutter contre la pollution réside bien évidemment dans les économies qu'elle permettra vraisemblablement de réaliser par rapport à l'application d'une réglementation contraignante. Les réglementations autoritaires imposent aux entreprises et aux ménages des coûts plus élevés, parce qu'elles sont généralement davantage basées sur la "disponibilité" ou "l'accessibilité" des techniques de lutte que sur l'efficacité au plan des coûts, et parce que les règles sont souvent les mêmes pour de grandes catégories de sources d'émissions. Ces deux facteurs expliquent pourquoi le coût marginal des mesures de lutte est extrêmement variable. Avec les instruments économiques, ce coût marginal est le même pour tous (il correspond soit au montant de la taxe sur les émissions, soit à celui du prix du permis d'émission) et, par conséquent, la lutte antipollution est globalement moins coûteuse.

Pour analyser les effets distributifs, il ne suffit cependant pas d'évaluer les économies globales. Pour déterminer à quels ménages la baisse des coûts bénéficiera en fin de compte, il faut savoir quelles seront les entreprises avantagées en la matière, puisque, comme nous l'avons déjà signalé, les incidences sur le prix des produits sont très variables d'un marché à l'autre. Les économies susceptibles d'être réalisées dans un secteur industriel donné sont fonction des coûts qu'il supporte dans le cas d'une réglementation contraignante et en cas d'application d'instruments économiques. Dans ce dernier cas, les coûts seront différents selon que les premiers permis d'émission sont ou non attribués en fonction des droits acquis et selon le montant de la taxe d'émission ou le prix des permis.

En somme, le cadre théorique proposé pour évaluer les incidences initiales et finales aux fins d'analyse des effets à long terme reprend une série d'étapes suivies depuis plusieurs années pour évaluer l'incidence d'autres programmes fiscaux. Au plan théorique, il n'y pas d'obstacles majeurs. En revanche, nous allons voir maintenant que, pour pouvoir employer cette méthode, il faut parfois disposer d'une quantité importante de données.

C. Analyse des effets transitoires

La figure 1 fait bien ressortir que, par rapport à une situation de "non-réglementation", l'application d'instruments économiques se traduit transitoirement par des coûts plus élevés pour les entreprises et pour les travailleurs. Les incidences initiales varient selon les secteurs. Ainsi, en cas de taxation des eaux polluées, les secteurs visés -- papeteries, usines chimiques, et autres entreprises effectuant des déversements importants -- vont avoir tendance à réduire leurs activités, voire à y mettre fin. Des personnes vont perdre leur emploi, et la valeur productive du capital va diminuer.

Ces effets transitoires sont généralement d'autant plus importants que la politique est appliquée dans des zones géographiques bien précises. Une taxe de déversement portant sur un seul cours d'eau risque de désavantager les entreprises riveraines vis-à-vis de la concurrence, avec pour conséquence un déclin potentiel de la production et de l'emploi dans la région concernée. De même, si un seul pays introduit une taxe sur les émissions, les secteurs dont les activités sont largement internationalisées vont être incités à transférer une partie de la production et des emplois vers d'autres pays, ce qui entraînera des coûts transitoires pour les entreprises et les travailleurs.

Quel sera l'impact de ces coûts transitoires sur les différents groupes, classés par niveaux de revenus ou en fonction d'autre critères ? Les effets des coûts supportés par les entreprises sur la répartition des revenus dépendront de la structure des revenus des actionnaires, exactement comme on a pu le voir à propos de l'analyse des effets à long terme. Les effets sur la répartition des revenus des travailleurs dépendront des changements relatifs de la demande de salariés à haut revenu et de salariés à faible revenu, et de leur mobilité relative.

L'approche comparative ne met pas aussi clairement en évidence la variation des coûts transitoires. On ne distingue pas très bien si les effets transitoires sont plus importants dans le cas d'instruments économiques ou dans le cas d'une réglementation contraignante. Nous avons signalé plus haut qu'il y avait deux effets contradictoires :

-- les instruments économiques font baisser le coût de *la lutte antipollution* et offrent une plus grande souplesse aux entreprises, ce qui atténue les effets transitoires, mais, d'autre part,

-- les instruments économiques créent des coûts d'opportunité pour les *émissions résiduelles* (soit directement, du fait du paiement des taxes ou des permis d'émission, soit indirectement, du fait de la possibilité de vendre les permis d'émission), ce qui tend à amplifier les effets transitoires. L'évaluation de l'impact net de ces deux effets contradictoires sur les coûts des entreprises (et donc sur les effets transitoires) est affaire d'empirisme.

IV. ETUDES EMPIRIQUES

Il existe relativement peu d'études empiriques sur les effets distributifs des programmes en faveur de l'environnement, et celles concernant les instruments économiques sont encore moins nombreuses. Le phénomène n'est pas difficile à expliquer. L'évaluation des schémas de répartition représente une tâche complexe. De plus, comme il n'existe pas de cadre largement admis pour structurer l'analyse, les différentes études qui ont pu être accomplies ne sont pas forcément comparables.

A. Quelques données empiriques

Ces dernières années, les propositions de taxes sur le carbone ont fait l'objet d'études qui ont fourni des informations sur les effets distributifs d'une telle taxe. Comme c'est le plus souvent le cas dans ce genre d'exercice, les études effectuées récemment ont été axées sur les tranches de revenus, mais certaines d'entre elles ont également fourni des indications sur les incidences en fonction d'autres regroupements en catégories, comme les secteurs industriels ou les régions géographiques. De plus, l'intérêt accru manifesté à l'égard des systèmes de permis d'émission négociables, notamment aux Etats-Unis, a été à l'origine de plusieurs études empiriques relatives à leurs répercussions sur la répartition des revenus.

1. *Politiques de l'environnement*

Les études empiriques sur la répartition des coûts des politiques d'environnement entre consommateurs et producteurs sont généralement conçues en termes d'équilibre partiel, suivant le modèle suivi pour analyser l'incidence de la fiscalité. On peut ensuite déterminer l'incidence de ces coûts pour les ménages, en fonction des tranches de revenus (ou d'autres catégorisations), d'après leur consommation de biens "taxés" et la part des charges supportées par les actionnaires qu'ils assument. Par exemple, Harrison (1974), a estimé pour les Etats-Unis les effets de la réglementation fédérale relative aux émissions des véhicules à moteur sur la répartition des revenus, en prévoyant l'évolution du prix des véhicules neufs et des véhicules d'occasion qu'entraîneraient les coûts induits par cette réglementation. Pour faire cette estimation, il s'est appuyé sur des données relatives à la structure des revenus des acquéreurs et des utilisateurs d'automobiles, à la structure des revenus des détenteurs d'actions et à la répartition de la charge fiscale. Il est apparu que le coût de la lutte contre les émissions des véhicules à moteur était régressif (c'est-à-dire qu'il était proportionnellement plus élevé pour les tranches de revenus les plus basses). D'autres études effectuées en Europe et aux Etats-Unis à propos du coût des mesures antipollution ont abouti à des conclusions similaires (cf. notamment Freeman, 1972, Peskin, 1978, Pearson et Smith 1991, Robinson, 1985). Toutefois, il peut être nettement moins régressif si, au lieu de se baser sur les revenus actuels, on se base sur les dépenses, représentatives des revenus à long terme (cf. Poterba 1991).

L'effet net dépend également de la répartition des avantages d'une politique d'environnement et de l'impact des coûts transitoires qu'une telle politique peut engendrer. En général, il semble que les catégories les plus démunies soient les premières à bénéficier concrètement de la lutte contre la pollution atmosphérique (en d'autres termes, l'évolution de l'exposition à la pollution est en moyenne plus importante pour ces catégories), parce que très souvent, les familles à faibles revenus sont regroupées au coeur des villes (cf. notamment Harrison, 1974, Zupan, 1973, ainsi que Asch et Seneca, 1979). Des disparités importantes sont cependant à noter d'une région à l'autre ; en général, pour les ménages à faibles revenus habitant dans des zones rurales, les avantages sont limités. De plus, pour les catégories moins favorisées, les gains ne sont pas aussi importants qu'on pourrait le penser eu égard aux améliorations physiques résultant de la lutte antipollution, dans la mesure où il s'opère un transfert partiel de ces gains des locataires vers les propriétaires, et parce que les ménages à faibles revenus attachent en général moins d'importance à la qualité de l'environnement. (cf. Harrison et Rubinfeld, 1978b).

Les effets distributifs des politiques d'environnement dépendent donc du résultat net obtenu par le jeu de plusieurs facteurs. Les études empiriques, relativement peu nombreuses, qui ont été menées jusqu'à présent portaient en général sur des points bien précis (par exemple, les effets distributifs des coûts liés aux mesures antipollution) plutôt que sur une évaluation plus globale.

2.   *Taxes sur les émissions*

Les travaux empiriques au sujet des taxes sur les émissions sont encore moins nombreux, même si, récemment, on pu noter plusieurs études à propos des taxes sur le carbone. L'étude de Pearson et Smith (1991) fournit des indications sur les effets distributifs que l'introduction d'une taxe sur le carbone pourrait avoir dans différents pays d'Europe. (Des études du même genre ont été menées en 1991 par Baker et Smith, ainsi que par Pearson). Des études détaillées ont révélé qu'au Royaume-Uni, une taxe sur le carbone de 10 $ par baril serait nettement régressive. En revanche, cette régressivité serait beaucoup moins prononcée dans d'autres pays d'Europe, où les dépenses en énergie et la consommation de combustibles à haute teneur en carbone ne sont pas les mêmes.

Il ressort d'un étude récente de la Banque Mondiale (Shah et Larsen, 1992) que, dans les pays en développement, l'incidence d'une taxe sur le carbone sur les coûts pourrait bien être fonction des revenus, et même qu'elle pourrait être progressive (en ce sens qu'elle frapperait plus lourdement sur les hauts revenus). Les calculs effectués pour le Pakistan font apparaître que, dans ce pays, une taxe sur le carbone serait proportionnelle aux revenus et que la charge qu'elle représenterait augmenterait parallèlement aux dépenses. De plus, si l'on tient compte du phénomène d'évasion fiscale et des autres imperfections qui caractérisent le système actuel d'impôt sur le revenu, on s'aperçoit que la progressivité de la taxe sur le carbone serait encore plus marquée.

Poterba (1991) laisse entendre qu'aux Etats-Unis, une taxe sur le carbone serait régressive, mais cette regressivité ne serait que marginale si on utilise les dépenses comme représentatives des revenus à long terme. Poterba précise que, comme d'autres auteurs, il n'a pas tenu compte d'un certain nombre d'éléments susceptibles de créer des complications, comme les effets liés à une situation d'équilibre général, les effets sur le marché des actifs, ainsi que les coûts au plan macro-économique et les coûts transitoires. De plus, il a fait abstraction du fait que les effets régressifs pourraient bien être atténués (voir ci après).

Plusieurs études ont été menées afin d'évaluer l'impact que l'introduction d'une taxe internationale sur le carbone aurait sur les économies nationales et sur l'économie mondiale. Hoeller et al. (1991) considèrent qu'une taxe internationale sur le carbone (exprimée en pourcentage) pèserait d'un poids beaucoup plus lourd sur l'économie des pays en développement ; ils prennent cependant soin de préciser que les résultats sont très sensibles à l'estimation des coûts. Vu le gaspillage énorme d'énergie auquel on assiste dans de nombreux pays en développement, il se pourrait que les possibilités de réduire à faible coût la consommation de combustibles à base de carbone soient plus importantes que ne l'indiquent les études actuelles. De plus, Whalley et Wigle (1990) ont montré que, suivant la structure adoptée, les incidences d'une taxe internationale sur le carbone pouvaient varier énormément d'une région à l'autre du monde.

3.   *Permis d'émission négociables*

Les études empiriques sur les permis d'émission négociables ont en général davantage analysé les incidences de tels systèmes pour différentes industries ou différentes régions que ses répercussions pour les diverses tranches de revenus. De plus, elles ont pratiquement toutes porté sur la situation des Etats-Unis; jusqu'à présent, les programmes fondés sur des permis d'émission négociables ont suscité beaucoup moins d'intérêt en Europe et dans les autres parties du monde (cf. Harrison et Nichols, 1990b).

Les problèmes de répartition des revenus se posent avec moins d'acuité avec les permis négociables, car on en apprécie généralement les effets par comparaison avec ceux obtenus en appliquant une réglementation contraignante ; comme, globalement, les coûts sont moins élevés, toutes les tranches de revenus sont avantagées; en fait, ceux qui retirent les plus gros avantages sont probablement ceux qui se situent dans les tranches de revenus les plus basses. (Comme nous l'avons noté plus haut, ce constat ne vaut peut-être pas si le coût d'opportunité se traduit par une augmentation des prix).

Des études révèlent que les programmes de permis d'émission négociables peuvent modifier très sensiblement la répartition géographique des emplois. C'est ainsi qu'aux Etats-Unis, le programme de permis négociables pour les émissions de substances provoquant des pluies acides devrait, selon les prévisions, se traduire par une augmentation de la production de charbon (et donc de l'emploi dans les mines) dans la partie ouest du pays, où se trouvent des gisements à faible teneur en soufre ; la production des régions de l'est, caractérisées par des gisements à forte teneur en soufre, devrait en revanche diminuer (ICF 1989a).

Les systèmes de permis négociables ont souvent la faveur des grandes entreprises, qui peuvent escompter en retirer des avantages substantiels en raison simplement de l'ampleur de leurs opérations et de leurs émissions. Les petites entreprises sont souvent plus circonspectes, d'une part parce qu'elles connaissent moins bien les instruments économiques et d'autre part parce qu'elles craignent que les grandes entreprises mettent le système à profit pour les évincer. Il s'agit d'un obstacle auquel l'Agence pour la protection de l'environnement des Etats-Unis s'est trouvée confrontée lorsqu'au milieu des années 80, elle a lancé un système de permis négociables pour réduire progressivement la teneur en plomb de l'essence (Harrison et Nichols, 1990b). L'expérience a cependant montré que ce système avait été profitable aussi bien pour les grosses raffineries que pour les petites, et qu'il n'y avait pas eu d'abus néfastes pour la concurrence (Hahn et Hester, 1989).

Le programme de permis négociables actuellement élaboré pour le bassin atmosphérique de la région de Los Angeles, en Californie, suscite le même genre d'objections de la part des petites entreprises. Ce programme a pour objectif de créer des marchés régionaux pour trois des principaux polluants affectant le bassin de Los Angeles (cf. South Coast Air Quality Management District, 1992). Une étude empirique a révélé que, par rapport aux résultats obtenus avec une réglementation contraignante, l'attribution de permis d'émission négociables ferait baisser d'au moins 40% le coût global de la lutte antipollution (Harrison et Nichols, 1992). D'après une étude de cas portant sur un petit secteur industriel, les petites entreprises retireraient probablement des avantages substantiels du passage à un système de permis d'émission négociables, à condition qu'on leur attribue au départ les mêmes droits d'émission que dans un système classique. Le secteur industriel choisi pour cette étude de cas se compose d'entreprises pour lesquelles le coût de la lutte antipollution est relativement peu élevé ; elles réaliseraient des bénéfices importants en revendant leurs droits d'émission à des entreprises ayant à supporter des coûts élevés en la matière. Toutefois, il ressort également de cette étude que, selon la méthode employée pour l'attribution des permis initiaux, les incidences pour les différentes industries pouvaient être extrêmement variables. Ce dernier point a également été souligné par d'autres auteurs. (cf. Harrison et Portney, 1982).

B.   Traits communs se dégageant des études empiriques

Un ensemble de traits communs semble se dégager des différentes études empiriques effectuées jusqu'à présent. Les principales conclusions sont les suivantes :

-- Le *coût* de la lutte contre la pollution est généralement régressif, en ce sens qu'il représente en pourcentage une charge plus lourde pour les ménages à faibles revenus que pour les ménages à revenus élevés.

-- Cette régressivité est moins nette lorsque les revenus sont mesurés d'après les dépenses (censées représenter les revenus à long terme) et non d'après leur montant actuel.

-- Si l'on se réfère aux changements d'ordre physique (évolution de l'exposition à la pollution atmosphérique, par exemple), les mesures antipollution *bénéficient* généralement aux catégories les plus démunies.

-- Le bénéfice pour les catégories les plus démunies est moins important s'il est exprimé en monnaie, car les ménages à faibles revenus semblent accorder moins d'importance à l'amélioration de la qualité de l'environnement que les ménages à hauts revenus.

-- Par rapport à une situation de non-réglementation, les taxes sur l'environnement tendent aussi à être régressives, mais le résultat final dépend de la manière dont les pouvoirs publics utilisent les recettes ainsi collectées.

-- Les taxes d'environnement et les systèmes de permis négociables peuvent être à l'origine d'importants transferts de richesses, le schéma de répartition dépendant dans une large mesure des caractéristiques du programme mis en oeuvre (par exemple, permis d'émission attribués par voie d'enchères ou en fonction des droits acquis et, dans le deuxième cas, formule d'attribution employée).

-- Les groupes peuvent se tromper quant aux répercussions qu'une taxe ou un système de permis négociables peut avoir sur eux.

-- Même relativement sommaire, une analyse des effets distributifs peut fournir des indications utiles quant aux gains et aux pertes.

La principale conclusion qui se dégage de ces études empiriques est peut-être que, pour pouvoir cerner clairement les enjeux réels de l'adoption d'instruments économiques, il faut soigneusement en analyser les effets distributifs. La démarche étant nouvelle, il est facile de se tromper sur les incidences que peuvent avoir des taxes sur les émissions et des programmes de permis d'émission négociables.

V. ATTENUATION DES EFFETS DISTRIBUTIFS

Si souhaitable que soit une politique, il y a pratiquement toujours des gagnants et des perdants. L'exemple le plus évident est celui des personnes qui perdent leur emploi pendant la période de transition entre deux politiques. Mais d'autres personnes peuvent également être perdantes. Même si, à long terme, les économies réalisées peuvent se traduire par une baisse des prix et par une augmentation de la production, il n'est pas exclu que certains prix augmentent du fait des taxes ou des "coûts d'opportunité". L'affectation des recettes éventuelles a également des incidences sur la structure des gains et des pertes.

En résumé, certains groupes subiront des pertes du fait de la mise en oeuvre de mécanismes d'incitation économique. Les groupes ainsi lésés feront vraisemblablement valoir qu'ils devraient obtenir des compensations.

A.   Faut-il payer des compensations ?

Pour deux raisons majeures, il apparaît nécessaire de prévoir des compensations à l'intention des victimes potentielles de la mise en oeuvre d'incitations économiques (Harrison et Portney 1982). La première relève du pragmatisme : si elles n'ont pas la perspective de recevoir des compensations, ces victimes potentielles risquent de bloquer l'adoption d'un système d'incitations économiques. Le risque de blocage est particulièrement grand si elles sont peu nombreuses et bien organisées alors que, par ailleurs, les gagnants sont largement disséminés et moins bien organisés.

La deuxième raison est en rapport avec les notions normatives d'équité : il est juste de prévoir des compensations si les victimes font partie des catégories sociales les plus démunies. Par exemple, ce critère, la mise au point de moyens de dédommager les catégories à faibles revenus se justifie si elles subissent des pertes d'emplois massives et de fortes hausses de prix. En somme, il peut être nécessaire de prévoir des compensations pour éviter que certaines couches sociales ne soient involontairement lésées, ou pour s'assurer un soutien politique.

Les deux raisons qui viennent d'être invoquées sont sujettes à caution. Des mesures compensatoires prises au coup par coup peuvent s'avérer insuffisantes eu égard à une vision plus large de l'équité, englobant l'ensemble des facteurs susceptibles d'affecter le bien-être des catégories nécessiteuses. Du point de vue politique, il est peut-être préférable de considérer que les réorientations de la politique de l'environnement font tout simplement partie des aléas auxquels sont soumis les profits des entreprises et le bien-être des ménages.

Nonobstant ces objections, il semble tout bien pesé important d'envisager des méthodes pour compenser les pertes subies du fait de la réglementation sur l'environnement, ou au moins d'admettre que les groupes perdants vont exercer des pressions afin d'obtenir des compensations. Il n'y a guère de raisons de penser qu'une politique globale de redistribution tiendra compte des effets distributifs résultant de la mise en oeuvre de mécanismes d'incitation économique ; il serait naïf d'imaginer que les groupes lésés ne feront pas état de leurs préoccupations dans le cadre du processus politique.

B.   Expérience acquise en matière de compensation

Il est nécessaire d'opérer une distinction entre atténuation et compensation. Par mesures d'atténuation, on entend les mesures prises *a priori* afin de réduire les effets potentiels d'un programme, de sorte qu'ils ne se produisent pas. Par exemple, les pouvoirs publics peuvent revoir à la baisse une certaine exigence en matière de lutte contre la pollution, voire y renoncer, pour ne pas nuire aux intérêts de certains groupes. Par mesures compensatoires, on entend les aides accordées *a posteriori* à certains groupes pour les dédommager (du moins en partie). Par exemple, les pouvoirs publics peuvent persister à imposer certaines mesures tout en sachant qu'elles seront néfastes pour l'emploi dans une région donnée, mais prévoir, à titre de compensation, des garanties de ressources et des programmes de formation.

Les politiques d'environnement mises en oeuvre dans les pays de l'OCDE offrent de nombreux exemples aussi bien de mesures d'atténuation que de mesures de compensation. Les prescriptions légales et réglementaires en matière d'environnement sont souvent établies en tenant compte de la capacité des entreprises d'un secteur industriel donné d'assurer le financement des équipements antipollution sans devoir cesser leurs activités ou restreindre fortement leur production. Les réglements sont conçus de manière à éviter les inconvénients et prévoient des normes moins rigoureuses pour ceux qui ont à supporter des coûts plus élevés, ce qui revient à atténuer les effets néfastes.

Les mesures compensatoires sont un autre trait commun des politiques d'environnement. Aux Etats-Unis, la fixation de normes fédérales de la qualité de l'air et de l'eau s'est assortie de programmes de subventions destinées à couvrir une partie des coûts. Ainsi, l'Agence pour la Protection de l'Environnement des Etats-Unis a accordé plus de 20 milliards de $ de subventions fédérales pour la construction de stations locales d'épuration des eaux. Un autre exemple de mesure compensatoire, largement inspirée par des considérations politiques, est la rémunération versée sur décision du Congrès américain aux bûcherons californiens privés d'emploi à la suite de l'extension du parc national Redwood à des zones précédemment exploitées.

Les mesures compensatoires ne sont nullement une particularité propre aux politiques d'environnement. Pour compenser les inconvénients de changements de politique, les pays de l'OCDE ont recours à différents programmes de garantie de ressources et de formation. Dans cet ordre d'idées, on peut citer les mesures d'aide à l'ajustement des entreprises ayant subi un préjudice, l'indexation des transferts en fonction de l'évolution des prix moyens, ainsi que les mesures d'allégement fiscal pour les entreprises ayant subi des pertes ou menacées de faillite.

C.   Moyens possibles d'atténuer les effets des instruments économiques

Il existe un certain nombre de moyens d'atténuer les pertes occasionnées par l'application d'instruments économiques. Dans tous les cas, l'objectif est d'essayer d'éviter les effets néfastes tout en maintenant les caractéristiques souhaitables du programme.

1.   *Taxes sur les émissions*

Un méthode apparemment simple pour atténuer les effets distributifs des taxes sur les émissions consisterait à réduire les recettes en fixant un seuil à partir duquel il serait procédé au prélèvement d'une taxe. Réduire les recettes fiscales en fixant un seuil n'est cependant pas aussi simple qu'on pourrait le penser (Harrison, 1989). Les seuils devraient être fixés non pas pour les émissions totales, mais pour chaque source d'émission, ce qui risque de poser des problèmes identiques à ceux rencontrés pour établir des normes d'émission différenciées. Si la base retenue pour la détermination des seuils est la même que pour la fixation des normes (c'est-à-dire les émissions par unité produite ou consommée), le système de taxes risque de perdre quelque peu de son efficience. En effet, les moyens employés pour inciter les entreprises à réduire leur production ou leur consommation ne seront pas les plus efficaces (Nichols, 1984). De plus, dans la pratique, il sera extrêmement difficile de trouver des seuils tels que tout paiement de taxe soit exclu, si bien qu'il y aura toujours un minimum d'effets distributifs.

Une autre méthode plus couramment employée pour atténuer les incidences de la fiscalité consiste à mettre en place un système d'exonérations comparable à celui qui existe dans certain pays pour les taxes indirectes sur les produits alimentaires et les articles d'habillement. Ainsi, la proposition de taxe sur le carbone de la Commission européenne prévoit la possibilité d'accorder des exonérations à un certain nombre de secteurs industriels gros consommateurs d'énergie, tels la sidérurgie et les cimenteries (Pearson et Smith, 1991). La Commission a proposé d'accorder ces exonérations compte tenu des effets néfastes que la taxe aurait sur la compétitivité internationale des secteurs précités, et elle suggère de les supprimer dès lors que les pays concurrents (notamment les

Etats-Unis et le Japon) adopteraient une taxe sur le carbone équivalente. En fait, ces effets néfastes sont le principal argument plaidant en faveur de l'élaboration à l'échelle mondiale d'une politique d'ensemble sur le carbone.

Il y a toutefois certaines raisons de mettre en doute l'opportunité d'une telle stratégie d'atténuation. Selon Pearson et Smith (1991), le fait d'accorder des exonérations comporte trois implications peu souhaitables. Premièrement, si l'on dispense certaines industries du paiement de la taxe, il faut, pour pouvoir atteindre les objectifs fixés en matière de réduction des émissions, taxer plus lourdement d'autres secteurs. Deuxièmement, en raison des exonérations, la structure de l'économie risque de se modifier et de s'orienter vers des activités polluantes, ce qui va à l'inverse de l'objectif défini lors de l'introduction de la taxe. Troisièmement (et c'est aux yeux de Pearson et Smith le point le plus important), les exonérations risquent fort de revêtir le caractère de mesures permanentes de protection. Pearson et Smith observent que l'on ne sait pas très bien en quoi pourraient consister des mesures répondant aux conditions requises pour l'abolition des exonérations. Introduire (pour atténuer les effets néfastes) des mesures permanentes de protection risquerait fort de compromettre la réalisation des objectifs poursuivis en matière tant de réduction au moindre coût des émissions polluantes carbone que de libéralisation des échanges.

2.   *Permis d'émission négociables*

Il est peut être plus facile d'élaborer des mesures propres à atténuer les effets des programmes de permis négociables, du moins ceux susceptibles d'affecter les entreprises, car, dans ce cas, il est possible de délivrer des titres de propriétés assortis d'une certaine valeur. Quelques-uns des effets distributifs de ces systèmes de permis négociables sont réduits, voire supprimés, par le jeu de mécanismes "naturels" (Harrison et Portney, 1982). En accordant les permis gratuitement, plutôt que par voie d'enchères, les pouvoirs publics peuvent épargner une perte globale aux entreprises. Les titres de propriétés sont partagés, et le droit de polluer détenu par les firmes dépend du nombre de permis accordés.

On peut employer une stratégie d'atténuation similaire lorsque les permis sont attribués par voie d'enchères, ce qui peut s'avérer souhaitable si on veut avoir l'assurance que les échanges se déroulent selon les règles de la concurrence et surmonter les réticences suscitées par ce genre de transactions. On peut mettre au point un système d'enchères ne procurant pas la moindre recette nette à l'Etat et éviter ainsi que des groupes importants ne soient lésés. Dans un tel système, les pouvoirs publics mettent les permis d'émission aux enchères, mais répartissent les recettes qui en sont retirées entre les participants (cf. Hahn et Noll, 1982). La formule employée pour l'organisation des enchères et pour la répartition des recettes est conçue de façon que toutes les attributions soient effectuées par voie d'enchères et que la redistribution opérée par les pouvoirs publics n'entre pas en ligne de compte lorsque les entreprises décident d'acquérir ou de vendre des droits d'émission.

Quelle que soit la formule retenue pour répartir les permis, il y a forcément des firmes gagnantes et des firmes perdantes. Les permis d'émission ont une certaine valeur. Les firmes vont donc être fortement incitées à soutenir les formules d'attribution qui leur permettent d'obtenir le maximum de permis. Ce qui est moins évident, c'est que la formule employée pour l'attribution des permis d'émission a des incidences sur le prix des produits, et donc sur la répartition des coûts entre les entreprises et les consommateurs, et qu'elle peut également entraîner des coûts transitoires pour les personnes privées d'emploi à la suite des ajustements opérés sur le marché (cf. Nichols et Harrison, 1991).

Si, pour attribuer les permis, on se base sur les activités antérieures (par exemple sur les émissions ou sur la production passées), le nombre de permis d'émission est fixe, et leur utilisation engendre un "coût d'opportunité". Ce coût se traduit sur le marché soit par des hausses de prix, soit par une diminution de la production. En revanche, si l'on se base sur les activités actuelles ou à venir, par exemple sur les émissions ou sur la production futures, il n'y a pas de coût d'opportunité, et les entreprises ne bénéficient pas d'une rente de situation. Cela signifie que les prix n'augmentent pas, et que la production ne diminue pas.

Il y a donc conflit entre la volonté d'assurer l'efficience du système de permis d'émission négociables et celle d'éviter les coûts transitoires (ou de plus larges répercussions sur les prix à la consommation). Si l'on attribue les permis en se basant sur les activités futures, on évite les effets transitoires et les incidences sur les prix, mais ce sera au détriment de l'efficacité du système : le prix des produits ne reflétera pas la valeur attachée à la réduction des émissions. A l'inverse, une politique efficace, consistant à attribuer les permis en se référant aux activités passées, peut entraîner des rentes de situation au profit de certaines entreprises, et avoir, en termes de production et de prix, des incidences néfastes pour certaines catégories.

Un autre obstacle à l'efficacité et à l'efficience d'un programme de permis d'émission négociables tient aux efforts déployés afin d'éviter le chômage en empêchant les firmes d'utiliser les ressources financières dégagées grâce à la fermeture d'unités de production. Des syndicats ont proposé que l'on interdise aux entreprises de se servir de ce genre de ressources. Toutefois, une telle politique serait pratiquement inapplicable dans la mesure où il serait à peu près impossible de déterminer quelles sont les entreprises ayant fermé des unités de production cause du système de permis négociables; il est fort probable que les entreprises contourneraient cette interdiction en maintenant des effectifs réduits au strict minimum. Tout porte donc à penser qu'une telle politique ne parviendrait pas à atténuer les effets négatifs. A supposer que l'on puisse ainsi éviter des licenciements, l'efficacité en ce qui concerne les coûts transitoires serait nulle, et les gains du point de vue de l'équité seraient coûteux.

D.   Compensation des effets induits par les instruments économiques

Les politiques de compensation peuvent être à l'origine de tensions similaires entre objectifs d'efficience et d'équité. Il est cependant possible de dédommager au moins un certain nombre d'individus pour les préjudices subis du fait du recours à des incitations économiques. Mais certaines mesures compensatoires peuvent compromettre la réalisation des objectifs de la politique d'incitation économique et engendrer d'autres problèmes du point de vue de l'efficacité et de l'équité.

1.   *Taxes sur les émissions*

La solution la plus courante pour compenser les effets distributifs d'une taxe consiste à faire en sorte qu'elle soit sans incidences sur les recettes, c'est-à-dire que l'on contrebalance l'augmentation des taxes sur les émissions en réduisant le montant d'autres taxes. Ainsi, dans sa proposition d'introduire d'une taxe sur le carbone, la Commission européenne souligne que cette taxe devra être sans incidences sur les recettes, (les recettes seraient reversées aux différents pays, qui seraient naturellement libres de choisir entre une diminution de la fiscalité et une augmentation des dépenses publiques). De la même manière, en Suède, l'introduction d'une taxe sur le carbone s'est inscrite dans le cadre d'une refonte du système fiscal, laquelle n'a pas eu d'incidences sur le volume global des recettes.

Comme nous l'avons noté, le code des impôts de nombreux pays comporte des dispositions qui permettent, dans le cadre des programmes de transfert de revenus, de compenser automatiquement certains effets grâce à l'indexation sur le niveau des prix. La compensation n'est cependant pas intégrale parce que tous les ménages à faibles revenus subissant ces effets ne bénéficient pas de transferts et parce que les dépenses d'énergie pèsent généralement plus lourd sur le budget des plus démunis (Poterba, 1991).

Le fait de réduire d'autres taxes afin que les taxes sur les émissions n'aient pas d'incidences sur les recettes peut être une source d'autres tensions entre les objectifs d'efficience et d'équité. Pearce (1991), ainsi que d'autres auteurs, ont déjà fait observer qu'un recours accru à des taxes sur l'environnement renforçait généralement l'efficience de la structure fiscale ; alors que les autres taxes sont une source de distorsions, celles sur l'environnement les diminuent. (Pearce parle à ce propos de "double dividende"). Terkla (1984) a évalué de manière empirique les gains d'efficience résultant du remplacement de toute une série de taxes couramment appliquées aux Etats-Unis par des taxes sur l'environnement. Pearson et Smith (1991) font état d'une étude récente selon laquelle, aux Etats-Unis, l'effet marginal de la structure fiscale sur le bien-être serait de l'ordre de 0,20 à 0,50 $ pour chaque dollar collecté. Toutefois, les taxes présentant les plus grandes distorsions ne sont pas celles qui pèsent le plus sur les couches démunies. Compenser l'augmentation des taxes sur le carbone par une diminution de l'impôt sur le revenu réduirait les distorsions au plan économique, mais ne contribuerait pratiquement pas à réduire la régressivité nette.

Il existe une foule de possibilités pour, à travers le système fiscal, compenser les effets régressifs (cf. notamment Poterba, 1991, ainsi que Pearson et Smith, 1991). Aux Etats-Unis par exemple, on pourrait augmenter les crédits d'impôt sur les revenus salariaux ou les abattements individuels, ce qui réduirait le poids de la fiscalité pour les ménages à faibles revenus (mais ne diminuerait pas les distorsions inhérentes au système fiscal). On pourrait également se servir de la législation fiscale pour compenser les charges pesant sur l'industrie, soit en réduisant l'impôt sur les sociétés, soit en accordant des avantages fiscaux aux entreprises installées dans des régions particulièrement touchées par la taxe sur le carbone.

Toutes ces modifications de la fiscalité posent un problème de ciblage. En d'autres termes, les bénéficiaires des mesures compensatoires ne sont pas forcément les individus et les ménages touchés par les taxes sur les émissions. Les aides accordées aux salariés ne sont pas d'un grand secours pour les personnes sans emploi. Les avantages consentis aux entreprises d'une région donnée profitent aussi bien à celles qui sont lourdement frappées par la fiscalité qu'à celles qui sont relativement peu touchées.

Un certain nombre de propositions ont été émises afin d'améliorer le ciblage des mesures compensatoires. Certaines de ces propositions ont trait à la fiscalité. Ainsi, Poterba (1991) suggère d'instituer un système explicite de crédits d'impôts pour les dépenses d'énergie. Le fait d'autoriser chaque ménage à déduire de ses impôts une somme correspondant à un certain pourcentage de la partie de ses revenus qu'il a consacrée à des dépenses d'énergie entraînerait un changement dans le prix moyen de l'énergie (et en atténuerait le caractère régressif), tout en maintenant l'efficience liée à un prix marginal plus élevé. Le lancement de programmes sur l'énergie en faveur des personnes âgées peut se justifier dans la mesure où, pour cette catégorie de la population, les frais de chauffage représentent un pourcentage plus élevé des revenus.

D'autres mesures pourraient être prises à l'intention des sans-emploi. On pourrait par exemple stimuler les créations d'entreprises dans les régions touchées, favoriser les migrations de main-d'oeuvre vers les régions où le marché de l'emploi est plus solide, lancer des programmes de formation afin de permettre aux travailleurs d'acquérir des compétences nouvelles, augmenter les dépenses publiques dans les régions, voire envisager la reprise des entreprises en difficulté. Même si certaines de ces mesures sont vraisemblablement efficaces du point de vue des coûts, l'expérience montre que les avantages que l'on en retire sont souvent relativement limités.

Aucune des mesures qui viennent d'être énoncées n'est parfaitement ciblée sur ceux qui sont touchés par les taxes sur les émissions. En fait, on peut, pour différentes raisons, ne pas souhaiter réaliser un ciblage parfait. Pourquoi une personne privée d'emploi à la suite de l'introduction d'une taxe sur le carbone devrait-elle faire l'objet d'un traitement fondamentalement différent de celui accordé à une autre ayant perdu son emploi pour une autre raison ? Dans la mesure où il est difficile d'appréhender les causes des pertes d'emplois, ce genre de comparaison est peut-être même impossible. Plutôt que de prévoir des mesures de compensation uniquement en faveur des personnes ayant subi des préjudices liés à une taxe, il est peut être préférable, pour des raisons d'efficience et d'équité, de mettre en place des programmes ayant une portée plus générale.

2.   *Permis d'émission négociables*

Dans la mesure où, en attribuant les autorisations en fonction des droits acquis et, en choisissant pour ce faire une formule appropriée, on peut *atténuer* les pertes des entreprises, le problème de la compensation des pertes subies par les entreprises ou les consommateurs se pose avec moins d'acuité dans le cas d'un système de permis négociables. Si l'on se place dans la perspective comparative qui domine la plupart des évaluations, il apparaît que les systèmes de permis négociables permettent d'économiser des coûts et de réduire les prix et jouent donc en faveur des plus démunis.

Toutefois, nous avons vu que la mise en oeuvre d'un système de permis négociables peut momentanément accroître le chômage. Les programmes visant à compenser les effets négatifs que des taxes sur les émissions peuvent avoir pour les travailleurs sont tout aussi valables dans le cas des permis négociables. Les problèmes d'efficience et de ciblage sont bien évidemment les mêmes.

VI. CADRE POUR L'ANALYSE DES EFFETS DISTRIBUTIFS

Il est indispensable de mettre au point un instrument pratique pour l'analyse des effets distributifs. Etant donné la complexité du sujet, les études pourraient être prolongées indéfiniment (et demeurer néanmoins incomplètes !). Pire encore, la tâche peut sembler ingrate au point de dissuader de se lancer dans la moindre étude formelle.

La présente section donne la liste des principaux points à prendre en considération lorsque l'on se prépare à analyser les effets distributifs des instruments économiques. Un certain nombre d'opérations empiriques sont à effectuer ; elles font l'objet d'explications plus détaillées.

A. Principaux points à prendre en considération

Nous avons mis l'accent sur le *cadre* dans lequel doit se dérouler l'analyse des effets distributifs des instruments économiques. Il est possible de transformer ce cadre en une liste de questions et de points à examiner. Les principaux éléments de cette liste sont les suivants :

1. Quelle est la *situation de référence* retenue pour les comparaisons ?

2. Les instruments économiques seront-ils une source de *recettes* publiques ?

3. Quelles sont les incidences *initiales* des instruments économiques ?

4. Sur quels *groupes* doit porter l'analyse des effets distributifs ?

5. Quelle est la *démarche empirique* à suivre pour déterminer les incidences *finales* (compte tenu des transferts d'avantages ou de coûts vers d'autres groupes) ?

6. Quels sont les moyens possibles d'*atténuer* ou de *compenser* les effets négatifs que le recours aux instruments économiques peut avoir pour différents groupes ?

La prise en compte de chacun de ces points, même si l'analyse est relativement sommaire, doit fournir la base d'une saine appréciation des effets distributifs.

B. Démarche empirique

De tous les points énumérés ci-dessus, celui autour duquel règne la plus grande confusion est peut-être le cinquième, à savoir la détermination de l'incidence finale des coûts et des avantages. En fin de compte, tous les coûts sont supportés par des particuliers. A la différence des actionnaires et des contribuables, les entreprises et les gouvernements ne supportent aucun coût. La détermination des coûts qui incombent en fin de compte aux particuliers implique toutefois une estimation de l'évolution des coûts des entreprises et des recettes publiques.

On peut proposer une démarche empirique pour l'estimation des effets à long terme et des effets transitoires. Cette démarche comporte les étapes suivantes :

1. Détermination, secteur industriel par secteur industriel, de l'évolution des coûts de mise en conformité (c'est-à-dire coûts de la lutte antipollution, plus coûts éventuels du paiement de taxes ou de l'acquisition de permis d'émission).

2. Détermination, secteur industriel par secteur industriel, des incidences de l'évolution des coûts de mise en conformité et de la prise en compte des "coûts d'opportunité" sur le prix des produits et sur la production.

3. Détermination des incidences de l'évolution des prix et de la production sur les "coûts transitoires" pour les travailleurs des zones géographiques considérées (c.à.d. nombre de personnes menacées à court terme de perdre leur emploi en raison des changements affectant la production dans leur région).

4. Détermination, d'après les données d'une enquête sur les dépenses, des incidences de la hausse du prix des produits sur la consommation des ménages dans les différentes tranches de revenus.

5. Détermination, secteur industriel par secteur industriel, des incidences de l'évolution des prix et de la production sur les bénéfices des entreprises.

6. Détermination de la manière dont les changements dans les bénéfices des entreprises sont ventilés entre les actionnaires et les contribuables (dans les pays prélevant un impôt sur les sociétés).

7. Assignation aux différentes tranches de revenus des changements affectant les actionnaires et les contribuables, d'après les données d'enquêtes sur la part que chacune d'entre elles représente dans les bénéfices des entreprises et dans l'impôt sur le revenu.

8. En cas de collecte de recettes publiques, identifier l'origine en termes de différentes tranches de revenus, d'après les mêmes données d'enquêtes indiquant la part de l'impôt sur le revenu payée par chaque tranche (si les recettes servent à réduire certaines taxes ou à financer de nouveaux programmes, il faut procéder différemment).

9. Faire, pour chaque tranche de revenus, la somme des résultats relatifs aux effets sur les prix, sur les actionnaires et sur les contribuables.

10. Faire la synthèse des résultats des analyses par tranches de revenus, pour les travailleurs et pour les différentes régions.

VII. CONCLUSIONS

Il ne fait pas de doute que les taxes sur le carbone et les autres instruments économiques vont pendant de nombreuses années encore figurer à l'ordre du jour des pays de l'OCDE. La décision de faire ou non appel à ces instruments dépendra d'un grand nombre de jugements portant sur les aspects scientifiques, économiques et politiques.

La présente étude est partie du principe selon lequel, il est important d'analyser les effets distributifs des instruments économiques. Une telle analyse répond essentiellement aux deux objectifs suivants :

1. Elle peut donner une idée plus précise des répercussions *réelles* que le recours aux instruments économiques pour faire face aux problèmes d'environnement peut avoir sur différents groupes.

2. Elle peut fournir des indications sur les stratégies que l'on peut *raisonnablement* envisager de mettre en oeuvre pour atténuer ces effets distributifs ou les compenser.

Ces deux objectifs sont liés. En précisant les répercussions réelles, on peut probablement montrer que bien souvent, les effets distributifs sont moins importants que ne le craignent certains et que, par conséquent, la nécessité de prévoir des mesures pour les atténuer est moins grande. En fait, comme la mise en oeuvre d'instruments économiques se traduit par une baisse du *coût global* de la protection de l'environnement, il est évident que l'abandon d'une réglementation contraignante de type classique ne peut être que bénéfique pour beaucoup.

Il est pratiquement impossible d'éviter *toutes* les pertes induites par la mise en oeuvre d'instruments économiques. Les taxes sur les émissions affectent plus durement certains consommateurs que d'autres, plus durement certains secteurs industriels que d'autres, et plus durement certaines catégories de salariés que d'autres. De même, bien qu'il soit largement admis que, par rapport aux méthodes contraignantes, les systèmes de permis d'émission négociables permettent d'économiser des coûts et ont moins d'incidences, on ne peut éviter que *certains* groupes se trouvent lésés.

Il semble cependant possible d'éviter que la mise en oeuvre d'instruments économiques se traduise par des difficultés majeures au plan de la redistribution. Les effets que les taxes sur les émissions exercent sur la répartition des revenus peuvent être compensés par des changements dans la législation fiscale. On peut concevoir, pour l'attribution initiale des permis d'émission négociables, des formules permettant de surmonter les principaux obstacles d'ordre politique. En cas de pertes d'emplois massives, on peut envisager des programmes de transfert ou de recyclage. Si les programmes d'incitation économique s'accompagnent de mesures destinées à en atténuer ou à en compenser les effets, ils peuvent être *à la fois* efficients et équitables.

RÉFÉRENCES BIBLIOGRAPHIQUES

ACKERMAN, Bruce A. et Richard B. STEWART. 1988. "Reforming Environmental Law : The Democratic Case for Market Incentives." *Columbia Journal of Environmental Law* 13:171-199.

ACKERMAN, Bruce A. et William HASSLER. 1981. *Clean Coal/Dirty Air*. New Haven : Yale University Press.

ALBERT, Alain 1991. "Cadre d'analyse des impacts redistributifs des mécanismes de type marché". Rapport préparé pour une réunion de Hauts Responsables du Budget à l'OCDE. Paris: OCDE, Juin.

ANDERSON, Frederick R. et al. 1977. *Environmental Improvement Through Economic Incentives*. Baltimore: The John Hopkins University Press for Resources for the Future.

ASCH, Peter et Joseph Seneca. 1979. "Some Evidence on the Distribution of Air Quality." *Land Economics.*

BAKER, Paul et Stephen SMITH. 1991. "Distributional Effects of Market-Based Environmental Policy Instruments in OECD Countries." Rapport préparé pour la Direction de l'Environnement de l'OCDE. Paris: OCDE, Novembre.

BARDE, Jean-Philippe. 1991. "Utilisation des instruments économiques pour la protection de l'environnement dans les pays de l'OCDE." Document présenté lors de la *Conférence Internationale sur l'Economie et l'Environnement dans les années 90*, 26-27 août.

BAUMOL, William J. et Wallace E. OATES. 1979. *Economics, Environmental Policy, and the Quality of Life*. Englewood Cliffs: Prentice-Hall, Inc.
-    1988. *The Theory of Environmental Policy*. New York: Cambridge University Press.

BOHM, Peter. 1991. "Taxation and Environment: The Case of Sweden." Document présenté lors de la *Réunion du Groupe de travail sur la fiscalité et l'environnement*. Paris: OCDE, 6-7 avril.

BRANNLUND, Runar et Bengt KRISTÖM. 1991. "Assessing the Impact of Environmental Charges: A Partial General Equilibrium Model of the Forest Sector." EFI Research Paper N° 6457. Stockholm, Novembre.

BURTRAW, Dallas et paul R. Portney. 1991. "The Role of Compensation in Implementing Market-Based Environmental Policies." Washington D.C.: Resources for the Future, Avril.

DALES, J.H. 1968. *Pollution, Property, and Prices*. Toronto: University of Toronto Press.

DAVID, Elizabeth. 1980. "Cost Effective Management Options for Attaining Water Quality." Rapport préparé pour le Department of Natural Resources Bureau of Planning. Madison, WI: DNR, Octobre.

DAVID, Martin et al. 1977. "Marketable Effluent Permits for the Control of Phosphorous Effluent in Lake Michigan." Document de travail du Social Systems Resarch Institute. University of Wisconsin, Décembre.

DELBEKE, Jos. 1991. "The prospects for the Use of Economic Instruments in EC Environmental Policy." Rapport présenté lors d'un séminaire du CEPS intitulé "*Setting New Priorities in EC Environmental Legislation*". Bruxelles : Commission des Communautés Européennes, Avril.

DENNY, Kevin et Stephen SMITH. 1991. "Methods for Quantitative Assessement of the Distributional Effects of Environmental Taxes." Rapport préparé pour la Direction de l'Environnement de l'OCDE. Paris, OCDE, Mai.

DE SAVORNIN Lohman, A.F. 1992. "Distributional Impacts of Environmental Charges". Rapport préparé pour le séminaire de l'OCDE consacré aux *Effets distributifs de l'utilisation des Instruments Economiques dans le cadre des Politiques d'Environnement*. Paris: OCDE, Avril.

DEWITT, Diane E, Hadi DOWLATABADI, et Raymond J. KOPP. 1991. "Who Bears the Burden of Energy Taxes?" Discussion Paper N° QE91-12. Washington DC: Resources for the Future, Mars.

DORFMAN, Nancy S. et Athur SNOW. 1975. "Who Will Pay for Pollution Control?" *National Tax Journal* 28(March): 101-115

FREEMAN, A. Myrick. 1972. "Distribution of Environmental Quality". Dans *Environmental Quality: Theory and Method in the Social Sciences*. A.V. Kneese et B.T. Bowers (éd). Baltimore, MD: Johns Hopkins University Press for Resources for the Future.

GIANESSI, Leonard P., Henry M. PESKIN et Edward WOLFF. 1979. "The Distributional Effects of Uniform Air Pollution Policy in the United States." *The Quaterly Journal of Economics* 93(2):281-301.

GOLDFARB, Robert S. 1980. "Compensating the Victims of Policy Change." *Regulation* 4(5):22-30.

HAHN, Robert W. et Gordon L. HESTER. 1989. "Marketable Permits: Lessons for Theory and Practice". *Ecology Law Quaterly* 16(2):361-406.

SHACKLETON, Robert et al. 1992. "The Efficiency Value of Carbon Tax Revenues." Projet de rapport préparé pour le Stanford Energy Modeling Forum 12. Washington, DC: U.S. Environmental Protection Agency, Energy Policy Branch, Mars.

SHAH, Anwar et Bjorn LARSEN. 1992. "Carbon Taxes, the Greenhouse Effect, and Developing Countries." Document de référence pour le *World Developemnt Report 1992*. Washington, DC : Banque Mondiale, Mars.

STAVINS, Robert N. 1988. *Project 88: Harnessing Market Forces to protect the Environment : Initiatives for the New President*. Washington, D.C.: Sénateurs Heinz et Wirth.

STAVINS, Robert N. et Bradley W. Whitehead. 1992. *The Greening of America's Taxes: Pollution Charges and Environmental Protection*. Washington, DC: Progressive Policy Institute, Février.

SOUTH COAST AIR QUALITY MANAGEMENT DISTRICT. 1991a. *Air Quality Assessement and Socio-Economic Impacts - "Implementation: Implications for the Basin."* Marketable Permits Program Working Paper N° 5. Los Angeles, CA: South Coast Air Quality Management District, Décembre.
- 1991b. *Draft Final 1991 Air Quality Management Plan, South Coast Air Basin*. Los Angeles, CA: South Coast Air Quality Management District and Southern California Association of Governments, Mai.
- 1992. *RECLAIM: Marketable Permits Program Summary Recommendations*. Los Angeles, CA: South Coast Air Quality Management District, Printemps

GROUPE DE TAVAIL SUR L'ENVIRONNEMENT ET LE MARCHÉ INTÉRIEUR. 1989. *1992; La Dimension environnementale*. Bruxelles : Commission des Communautés Européennes.

TERKLA, D. 1984. "The Efficiency Value of Effluent Tax Revenues." *Journal of Environmental Economics and Management*.

TIETENBERG, Thomas H. 1985. *Emissions Trading, An Exercise in Reforming Pollution Policy*. Washington, DC, Resources for the Future.

CONGRÈS DES ETATS-UNIS. 1990. *Carbon Charges as a Response to Global Warming : The Effects of Taxing Fossil Fuels*. Washington, DC: Congressional Budget Office, Août.

WEITZMAN, Martin. 1974. "Prices vs. Quantities." *Review of Economic Studies* 41(October): 477-491.

WHALLEY, John et Randall WIGLE. 1990. "The International Incidence of Carbon Taxes". Rapport soumis lors de la Conférence organisée à l'Istituto Bancario Sao Paolo di Torino sur le thème *Economic Policy Responses to Global Warming*, Palazzo Colonna, Rome, Octobre.

Chapter 1

Introduction

Governments throughout the world are facing increasing pressure to solve environmental problems and in the process, they are confronting the need to develop a consensus among groups with very different views. These differing views reflect in part the fact that any policy choice inevitably leads to different impacts on different groups. Those who lose—or believe that they may lose—are likely to resist. The result can be paralysis or mediocrity.

Agreement on solutions to environmental problems is particularly difficult partly because they often transcend narrow political boundaries. Local groups can often agree on solutions to crime, education, and even health care. But many environmental problems are harder to confine. Rivers flow. Air masses move. Decisions to clear forests or emit greenhouse gases affect the temperature of the entire globe.

These difficulties would be much less prominent if the stakes were not so high. Global warming, biological diversity, loss of the ozone layer, proliferation of toxic substances, acid rain, urban smog, loss of wetlands—solutions to these and other environmental problems may be very expensive. Estimates of the cost of reducing greenhouse gas emissions range from one to three percent of gross domestic product. These and other costs would add to the one to two percent of their gross domestic product that many OECD countries now devote to environmental programmes.

A. Policy approaches for environmental protection

Economic instruments are gaining greater support among policy makers and others as means of dealing with these environmental problems because they promise to reduce the costs and add flexibility in environmental policy. The Council of the Organisation for Economic Co-operation and Development (OECD) in January of 1991 adopted a resolution recommending that Member countries "make a greater and more consistent use of economic instruments . . ." (OECD 1991a, p. 3). That resolution reflected the increasingly large number of actual examples and policy proposals. Prominent examples include global carbon tax and carbon trading programmes proposed in many international forums, the carbon tax programmes proposed or enacted in individual Scandinavian and European countries, and the acid rain trading programme recently adopted in the United States.

These strategies promise to lower the cost of meeting air quality targets by 40 percent or more compared to the traditional "command-and-control" approach. The traditional approach involves setting individual emission standards for sources in various key source categories, such as power plants or oil refineries. Uniform standards are set for all sources within these categories, with the standards typically set on the basis of the availability of control technology. Uniform standards do not mean uniform costs, however; the same technology can lead to vastly different costs per ton controlled. The result is that technology-based emission standards can lead to relatively high costs for achieving environmental goals because there is no mechanism to concentrate emission control where it can be accomplished most cheaply.

This technology-based approach also tends to freeze pollution control technology because firms have no incentives to find techniques to reduce pollution below standards. Indeed, uncovering such techniques may simply lead to more stringent emission standards, implying negative incentives to develop new technology. Emission taxes or emissions trading strategies, in contrast, reward firms for finding cheaper and more effective means of reducing emissions. The net result of switching to economic instruments is thus lower costs both in the short term and the long term.

Lower overall costs do *not*, however, guarantee agreement to adopt a tax or trading programme. Like all policies that improve *overall* welfare, economic instruments might be blocked by those who believe they might lose. Indeed, because they are novel, economic instruments face even greater hurdles than traditional "command-and-control" strategies whose basic features have been honed for decades in most OECD countries.

These considerations mean that proponents of economic instruments need to consider the *distributive* impacts of economic instruments as well as overall gains. Thus far, much less attention has been paid to these effects. Two questions emerge:

1. Who gains and who loses from the use of economic instruments?

2. What, if anything, should be done to reduce any negative impacts?

Answers to these questions put policy makers in a position to deal with the complexities of reaching agreement in high-stakes policy arenas.

B. Purpose of this study

The primary purpose of this study is to provide a systematic framework that can be used to estimate distributive effects.[1] The premise is that assessing who gains and who loses is a *precondition* for negotiating and reaching agreement on whether to use economic instruments and on how to design the programmes. The study does *not* provide recommendations on whether or not economic instruments should be used, either by themselves or in conjunction with other policy instruments.

Developing a framework for distributive analyses of economic instruments involves several issues. It is useful to think of these issues as falling into five distinct stages. Although much of the political discussion of environmental (and other) policies revolves around impacts on one group or another, there is virtually no consensus on what a distributional analysis should include and how it should be conducted. The first stage, therefore, is to address "threshold" issues that precede the formal analysis and data collection. These threshold issues include determining the benchmark for evaluating economic instruments as well as specifying the groups whose impacts are to be estimated.

The second stage is to provide a conceptual framework for the analysis. Standard microeconomic tools can be used as the backbone for this conceptual framework — as they have been used for many years in tax incidence analysis — although there are a number of complications that arise. Perhaps the most important complication is the usefulness of considering *transitional* impacts on workers and others, which are typically ignored in most long-term microeconomic modelling. The result of this somewhat expanded conceptual framework is a set of steps that can be used to develop empirical estimates of distributive impacts.

The third stage involves empirical estimation. To illustrate the range of possible empirical studies, this study summarizes the relatively sparse empirical evidence on distributive impacts. This evidence includes studies of environmental policies that rely on traditional regulation as well as those dealing with economic instruments.

The fourth stage is to assess the options for mitigating any negative effects. All policies lead to some losers, regardless of how large their overall net benefits. (The distributive analysis is likely to show, however, that some groups' concerns are not justified.) It is useful to distinguish policies that prevent the adverse impacts from occurring from those that compensate groups after the fact. The study refers to the former policies as mitigation and the latter policies as compensation. The objective of any mitigation or compensation strategy is to avoid harms without compromising the major advantages of the economic incentive strategy.

The fifth and final stage is to bring these various elements together into a "checklist" of key issues. The purpose of the checklist is to provide a construct that can be used by policy analysts to develop distributive analyses for economic incentive proposals.

C. Organization of the report

The remainder of this study is organized as follows. Chapter 2 provides background on economic instruments. Chapter 3 provides the initial framework for distributive analysis, including a discussion of the "threshold" issues as well as a structure that lays out the key threshold choices. Chapter 4 describes the conceptual framework for analysing the distributive consequences of economic instruments on a given group, taking into account both the long-term impacts and possible transitional impacts. Chapter 5 summarizes the existing empirical evidence on distributive effects, both of environmental programmes and economic instruments. Chapter 6 provides a discussion of policy choices to mitigate or compensate for adverse distributive impacts. Chapter 7 provides the final "checklist" and some concluding remarks.

It is useful to provide an illustration of how a distributive analysis might be carried out. The Appendix provides a detailed case study of some of the distributive impacts of the emissions trading programme being developed for the Los Angeles air basin.

Chapter 2

Background on Economic Instruments

Economic instruments constitute a class of policy tools that can be used to achieve environmental goals. Their purpose is to influence the behaviour of emitters by providing an economic (rather than a purely legal) incentive to reduce pollution. Economic instruments thus put a "price" on pollution as a means of achieving reductions. This chapter discusses the economic instruments addressed in this study and provides an overview of their logic and basic characteristics. The chapter ends with a summary of the experience with economic instruments in OECD countries.

A. Economic instruments considered in this study

A wide variety of policies have been called economic instruments in particular, hazardous product labelling, environmental liability and damage compensation schemes, and deposit refund schemes. (See OECD 1991c for a recent summary of various types of economic instruments and guidelines for their application.) This report focuses on two major types of economic instruments: emission taxes and emissions trading.

1. Emissions taxes

Emission taxes are levied on the discharge of pollutants into the air, water, and soil, and on the generation of noise. Their calculation is based upon the quantity (and sometimes the quality) of the pollutant emitted. They can be contrasted to two similar charging schemes: user charges and product charges.[2] User charges, such as those for public water treatment facilities, are designed primarily to collect revenue to cover the cost of public facilities. Product charges are levied on products that are harmful to the environment such as pesticides, detergents, fuels and the like. The objective of product charges is to reflect the unregulated "life-cycle" environmental costs of the production and use of various products.

This study focuses on emission taxes (or emission charges in some studies) because, unlike most other mechanisms which are designed to raise revenues, emission taxes provide incentives for reaching environmental goals at the lowest cost. Since other charge schemes resemble emissions taxes in certain respects, they can replace emission taxes when it is not feasible to directly tax emissions. Most of the conceptual framework presented in the following chapters can be used for assessing the distributive impacts of these other mechanisms as well.

2. Emissions trading

Emissions trading programmes are similar to emissions taxes in their ability to encourage cost-effective emission control. The difference is that while taxes set the price and allow the reactions of emitters to determine the quantity of emissions, trading schemes set the quantity of emissions and allow the market for emissions allowances (i.e., the right to emit a unit of the pollutant) to determine the price. Under conditions of certainty regarding control costs, the two approaches are equivalent. Choosing one or another approach depends upon a variety of factors.[3]

A range of terminology has been used to describe these programmes (see OECD 1991d): marketable permits, tradeable permits, credit systems, or averaging systems. The units of exchange are referred to as credits, allowances, or marketable permits. Although there are some differences in the details of various trading programmes, the underlying characteristic is that firms (or individuals) can trade the right to emit a quantity of pollution. This study uses the term emissions trading to refer to all of these programmes and the term emission allowance to describe the unit of exchange.

B. The logic and mechanism of economic instruments

Environmental policy can be thought of as consisting of two interrelated decisions. The first is to choose the overall goal, such as the level of air quality in an air basin or the level of water quality on a river. The second is to determine the means (or "instrument") for achieving a given goal. Economic instruments are means of achieving policy goals and in many cases are neutral with respect to the goals themselves.[4]

1. Command-and-control emission standards

Most environmental regulation in OECD countries is accomplished through what are usually referred to as "command-and-control" standards. These standards are typically uniform for all sources within a given category. The choice of precise standards is based on the availability and effectiveness of emission control technologies and their affordability for firms within the source category (see OECD 1989 and Portney 1990). In the United States, for example, the underlying logic in setting emission standards is that controls should be as tight as technology allows (particularly with new plants), without creating visible economic dislocations such as plant closures and major job losses. Note that neither of these criteria take into account the cost-effectiveness of emission controls, as measured by the cost per unit of emission controlled.

The command-and-control approach to environmental regulation inevitably leads to unnecessarily high costs, both because it tends to freeze pollution-control technology and because it leads to wide disparities in the incremental costs of controlling pollution. Empirical studies show that the cost differences can be very large. For example, an analysis of the marginal cost of removing oxygen-demanding organic material found a thirtyfold range of marginal costs within six industries studied (Magat, Krupnick and Harrington 1986). (Marginal cost in this context refers to the incremental cost of removing the last ton of pollutant.) The marginal cost of controlling a given air pollutant can differ by a factor of 100 or more among sources, depending upon the age and location of the plant and the available technologies (Crandall 1983). Such wide variations create opportunities to decrease overall control costs substantially by using economic instruments.

2. Cost savings from emissions taxes and emissions trading

A simple example shows the basic way in which economic instruments can reduce control costs. Figure 1 illustrates a hypothetical situation in which two plants incur very different marginal costs in meeting the same standard. Plant I incurs a marginal cost of only $500 per ton controlled, while Plant II spends $3,000 for the last ton controlled. These two sources could be different plants within the same company, plants owned by different companies within the same industry, or sources in completely different industries. One source, for example, might be a boiler in an electric utility plant and another might be an oil refinery.

Figure 2. **Emission standards often lead to large differences in marginal costs**

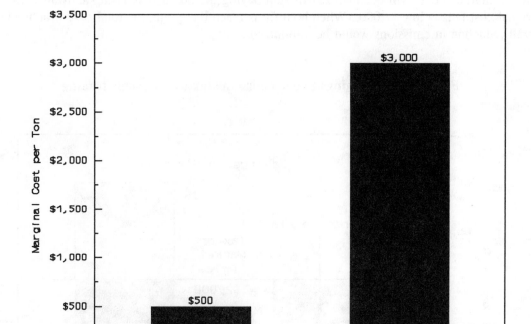

The same overall reduction in emissions could be achieved at lower compliance costs by tightening controls at Plant I and relaxing them at Plant II. Relaxing controls at Plant II by one ton saves $3,000, while capturing that additional ton at Plant I raises costs by only $500, for a net saving in compliance costs of $2,500.

45

? shows how these cost savings would be achieved if an emissions tax or emissions trading programme were in place. The example assumes that both the emissions tax and the price established in the market for emissions allowances would be $2,000 per ton. The owner of Plant I (the low-cost source) would respond to either the tax or trading scheme by controlling the additional ton. Controlling the ton would cost $500 while the firm would save $2,000 by not paying the tax or purchasing the allowance.[5] The net savings would be $1,500. In contrast, the owner of Plant II (the high-cost source) would pay the tax or purchase the allowance. Control costs would be reduced by $3,000, for a net savings of $1,000 in comparison with the $2,000 spent to pay the tax or purchase the allowance.

How far will such cost-reducing transactions proceed? As Plant I controls more in order to avoid the tax or the need to buy permits, its marginal cost is likely to rise. (Most empirical studies show that the marginal cost of controlling emissions rises as the level of emissions is reduced.) The plant will stop controlling emissions at the point at which the additional controls would cost $2,000. The situation is just the reverse for Plant II. As it relaxes controls more and more, its marginal cost will decline. It will stop paying the tax or purchasing allowances when its marginal cost falls below $2,000. When both firms reach that point, the total cost of achieving the overall reduction in emissions would be minimized.

Figure 3. **Cost savings under emissions tax or emissions trading**

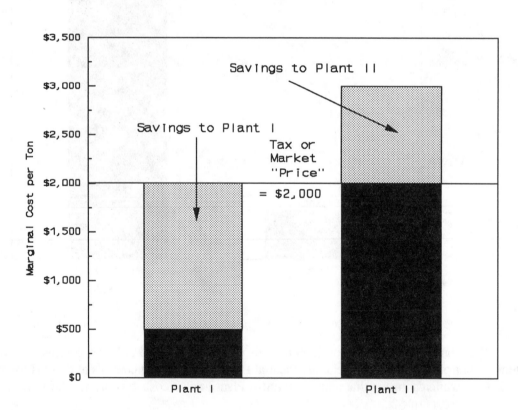

46

3. Incentives to develop emissions control technology

These simple examples assume that the cost of controlling emissions remains the same with economic instruments. However, putting a price on emissions will provide economic incentives to develop cheaper means of controlling emissions. As noted above, emission standards can actually retard the development of emissions control technology, because of the possibility that new cost-saving approaches would simply lead to additional requirements.

The possibility of lower-cost control means that the overall cost savings from economic incentives could be substantially greater than the simple example illustrates. These long-run considerations could be even more important than the short-run cost savings based upon current technological control options (see Downing and White 1986 and Milliman and Prince 1989). They are, however, difficult to quantify.

4. Payments to government

The above example ignores the possibility that firms operating under economic instruments would make payments to the government. Such payments are an important element of a distributive analysis of economic instruments, and they are analyzed in detail in subsequent chapters of the study. However, government revenues are not likely to have a major impact on the *overall* gains to society from economic instruments. The revenues are a transfer from firms (or their customers) to the government. The government would use the added revenues either to lower other taxes or pay for additional government services. There is no social cost incurred by the transfer.[6]

The government could collect revenue from either emission taxes or emissions trading programmes. Firms would pay taxes for any emissions that remain after cost-effective controls are in place. Firms would pay under the emissions trading programme if the government auctioned the emissions allowances initially. However, if the allowances were distributed to firms through a "grandfathering" arrangement, the government would not collect revenues under the emissions trading programme.

C. Overview of experience with emissions taxes and emissions trading

This section provides an overview of how emissions tax and trading strategies have been put into practice in recent years, dealing first with taxes and then with trading.

1. Experience with Emissions Taxes

Taxes or charges related to environmental concerns have become increasingly common in many OECD countries in recent years. However, virtually none of the existing tax programmes is designed as a substitute for emission standards in the sense of providing incentives to reduce pollution. To provide appropriate incentives to reduce pollution (and minimize control costs) the tax should have two characteristics:

- the tax should be based upon the amount of pollution produced (or a close proxy), so that the charge to a firm would be reduced if it generated less pollution;[7] and

- the tax should be large enough to reflect the marginal damages from emissions; small pollution charges will simply raise revenue rather than reduce pollution, particularly if they are imposed in concert with a tight standard.

Most of the charge schemes that are now in place are in fact modest taxes on polluting products that are designed to raise revenues—typically to cover the cost of public treatment or other public expenditures—rather than to provide incentives to reduce pollution and to minimize compliance costs. However, this situation appears to be changing, particularly in Scandinavia and Europe, as the number of "green taxes" (including carbon taxes) increases.

a) Overview of OECD survey of emissions taxes

In 1989, the OECD published a survey of experience with emission taxes and other economic incentives in fourteen OECD countries. The survey distinguished the following different types of tax or charge schemes:

- *Effluent charges* are charges to be paid based upon the quantity (or quality) of the discharged pollutants;

- *User charges* are payments for public treatment facilities (typically water effluent treatment) that might differ according to the amount of effluent;

- *Product charges* are charges based upon the potential pollution of the product;

- *Administrative charges* are payments for government services (e.g., registration of chemicals, implementation and enforcement of regulations); and

- *Tax differentiation* leads to more favourable prices for "environmentally friendly" products, and is thus similar to product charges except that the tax differentiation option is usually not designed to raise net revenue. As noted above, this study concentrates on emissions taxes, the first category in this list. However, it is useful to consider the experience with all of these various tax or charge schemes.

Table I lists the conclusions of the OECD survey regarding the prevalence and performance of these tax mechanisms as of 1987. The list distinguishes between their stated purpose and their practical effect. The authors determined whether the schemes were designed to have incentive effects on pollution or whether they were designed to raise revenue, and how they worked in practice.

This table indicates that a small number of charge schemes have incentive effects, but that the bulk of the schemes have been designed with financial (i.e., revenue-raising) objectives in mind. Virtually all of the emission tax schemes (labelled effluent charges in Table I) are not true economic instruments because the level is not set high enough to influence firms' decisions. Indeed, even the German tax scheme—which is the only tax strategy that is both designed to encourage cost-effective control and actually achieves that purpose in practice—actually operates as a supplement to conventional "command-and-control" regulations (see Harrison and Nichols 1990b and OECD 1991d).

Table I. Evaluation of the Purpose and Practice of Charge Schemes in OECD Countries

	Purpose: Incentive	Purpose: Incentive	Purpose: Financial	Purpose: Financial
	Practice: Incentive	Practice: Financial	Practice: Financial	Practice: Incentive
Effluent Charges				
Air		France		
Water	Germany	Italy	France	Netherlands
Waste	Denmark	Belgium	United States	
Aircraft Noise			France Germany Japan Netherlands Switzerland	
Industrial Noise			United Kingdom Netherlands	
User Charges			All Countries	
Product Charges				
Lubricants			Finland France Germany Italy Netherlands	
Mineral oil and products		Norway	Finland Netherlands Sweden	
Beverage containers	Finland	Sweden[1]		
Food containers	Norway			
Batteries		Sweden[1]		
Fertilizers		Sweden[1]		
Pesticides		Sweden[1]		
Feedstock			United States	
Administrative Charges				
Waste			Belgium	
Pesticides	Sweden		Denmark Finland	
Chemicals	Sweden			
Tax differentiation	All countries			

Note: [1]These Swedish product charges have a stated financial purpose as well.
Source: OECD (1989, Table 3.17).

b) Recent developments

The role of emissions taxes seems likely to grow as environmental considerations become increasingly important and as economic incentives become more widely discussed. Much of the current discussion concerns the use of greenhouse taxes to deal with global warming, although emission taxes are also being proposed to deal with other air pollutants as well as with solid waste and noise.

The list of recent actual or proposed emissions taxes and similar mechanisms in OECD countries is lengthy. It is useful to provide some examples of the types of tax programmes being considered. (See Harrison and Nichols 1990b, Barde 1991, Carlin 1992 and Stavins and Whitehead 1992 for more information on these initiatives.)

Most of the recent environmental tax programmes and proposals have been developed in Scandinavia or Europe. (See Delbeke 1991 for a discussion of policy statements and positions regarding environmental taxes on the part of the Commission of the European Communities.) The following examples are intended to provide the flavour for these various proposals. Sweden has included environmental taxes as part of a general reform of the tax system that includes a tax on carbon dioxide and sulphur. The Swedish government is currently evaluating the performance of the various economic instruments used in Sweden, including analyses of the potential effect of the policies on industrial competitiveness. Norway, Denmark and Finland have also instituted "green taxes" in recent years. The range of taxed products includes pesticides, chlorofluorocarbons (CFCs), waste oil, and phosphate fertilizers. France is considering redesigning water charges to discourage farmers from using nitrate fertilizers. Italy has instituted a tax on plastic bags. In Belgium, proposals to tax waste water and solid waste and being debated, while Switzerland is studying taxes on fertilizers, fuels, and various sources of hydrocarbon emissions.

The United States has not had as much experience as European or Scandinavian countries with "green taxes," perhaps because of the lesser importance of excise taxes in the United States (Harrison and Nichols 1990b). Indeed, although the United States has introduced a tax on CFCs, the tax was primarily designed to avoid the large wealth transfers created by the initial emissions trading programme. However, environmental tax policies are being increasingly discussed as policy options; more than a dozen bills have been introduced in the Congress in recent years to tax substances ranging from air pollution emissions to polystyrene packaging. In addition, the 1990 Clean Air Act includes a number of provisions for environmental taxes, including a fee on volatile organic compound (VOC) emissions of $5,000 per ton (annually adjusted for inflation). The tax would be imposed on major stationary sources—applying to emissions above 80 percent of a baseline level—located in air basins that did not meet federal timetables for achieving air quality targets (see Carlin 1992 and Elman et al. 1992).

Several ongoing OECD studies are monitoring global warming tax proposals in OECD countries. Five countries have already introduced greenhouse taxes. These five include Denmark, Finland, Norway, Sweden, and the Netherlands. Greenhouse taxes have been discussed in many other OECD countries. In addition, the European Commission recently adopted a proposal for a directive that would introduce a CO_2/energy tax, coupled with tax incentives for investments in energy savings or CO_2 abatement.

These various carbon tax programmes and proposals differ considerably in a number of important respects, including the products included in the tax base, the tax rate, exemptions, and timetable for implementation. The European Commission proposal represents an attempt to develop consistency. The tax would be determined and established at the Community level, but the arrangements for charging and collecting it would be left to the member states, with the tax receipts going to the individual countries.

2. Experience with emissions trading

Most of the experience with emissions trading in OECD countries has been concentrated in the United States. There are, however, a number of important initiatives in other OECD countries. In addition, various international organizations (including the OECD) are considering the possibility of developing an emissions trading programme to deal with global warming.

a) Experience in the United States

The experience with emissions trading in the United States can be viewed as progression from circumscribed policies that are grafted onto traditional command-and-control regulatory systems to full-fledged emissions trading programmes that represent a true alternative to traditional regulation. This progression ranges from the "emissions trading" (or ET) programmes developed by the United States Environmental Protection Agency in the late 1970's to the acid rain trading programme passed as part of the 1990 Clean Air Act.[8]

Emissions trading (ET) programmes

The 1970 Clean Air Act set national ambient air quality standards for ambient pollutants, such as ozone and particulate matter. Achieving these standards is a joint responsibility of the federal government and the states, with emission standards for new sources set nationally and emissions from existing sources set by the states. The inflexibility of the resulting set of emission standards led to several programmes designed to provide some flexibility. These are generally referred to collectively as "emissions trading" (or "ET") programmes.

The most well-known ET programme is the "bubble" policy, in which firms are allowed to combine standards for several sources into one overall limit; the name evokes the image of placing an imaginary bubble over several individual stacks and then measuring the sum of the emissions rather than the individual stack emissions. The three other ET programmes are: (a) netting, in which new sources are exempted from review if existing emissions are reduced enough to yield no net increase; (b) offsets, in which a major new source is allowed to locate in an area not meeting ambient standards if it obtains offsetting reductions from its own facilities or other facilities; and (c) banking, in which a firm is allowed to "bank" emissions below the standard for future use as an offset or other purpose.

Experience with the ET programmes has yielded mixed results. Hahn and Hester (1989) estimate that overall cost savings through 1986 were approximately $1 billion, less than 1 percent of the overall air pollution expenditures over the period. The primary problems are that ET has imposed many restrictions on allowable trades and set procedural requirements that have raised the

51

cost of trades and created uncertainty and delay (see Dudek and Palmisano 1988 and Harrison and Nichols 1990b for evaluations of the ET programme). The net result is that the promise of the ET programme has been far greater than its performance.

Lead trading in gasoline

The approach used to regulate lead in gasoline during the 1980's offers a more successful example of the use of emissions trading. The United States Environmental Protection Agency regulates the amount of lead in gasoline, both to reduce airborne concentrations of lead and to avoid poisoning the catalysts used in auto emission control systems. In 1982, these regulations were amended to allow refiners to trade lead credits among themselves. Under these new rules, a refinery could produce lead above the limit if it purchased a sufficient number of lead rights from refineries that produced lead below the limit. In 1985, the Environmental Protection Agency promulgated a rule to reduce the lead limit by more than ten-fold. At the same time, a banking provision was added that allowed refineries to "bank" lead rights for future use.

Although refiners were originally sceptical of the value of trading—expressing some concerns that trading would be used by the large refiners to drive smaller refiners out of business—the programme proved very popular. In a typical quarter, more than half of the refineries participated in the market. By 1987, more than 50 percent of the lead in gasoline was traded. No overall cost saving estimates are available; but the Environmental Protection Agency estimated the cost savings from banking alone to be about 20 percent of the cost of the programme. The programme appears to have been successful because—in contrast to the ET programme—the property rights for lead rights were secure and administrative red tape was minimized.

Chlorofluorocarbons (CFC's)

As part of its implementation of the Montreal Protocol on Substances that Deplete the Ozone Layer, the United States in 1988 set up an emissions trading programme to phase out the use of CFC's. Firms producing CFC's were allocated allowances on the basis of historical domestic production and imports, with firms free to trade the allowances among themselves. As noted above, in 1989 Congress passed a tax on permits designed to recover some of the value captured by CFC manufacturers as a result of price increases for CFC's.

No estimates have been made of the cost savings from this precise emissions trading programme. However, an earlier study estimated that an emissions trading programme would cost about 50 percent less than an equally effective system of mandatory controls (Palmer et al. 1980). That study also concluded that a trading scheme would lead to even greater savings in the long run due to its inducement of innovations for cost-effective emissions reductions.

Acid rain trading programme

The emissions trading programme to control SO_2 emissions from electric utility power plants is the most prominent emissions trading programme. It establishes a national cap on total power plant emissions of 8.9 million tons by the year 2000, roughly a 50 percent reduction from current levels. Electric utilities are allocated allowances to emit SO_2 based primarily on historical emissions (i.e., the allowances are "grandfathered"). The utilities are allowed to trade SO_2 allowances across plants and across utilities. Furthermore, non-utilities are given the opportunity to "opt in" to the trading programme. The programme allows for the "banking" or carryover of unused allowances. In addition, a small number of allowances (2.8 percent of the total) are set aside by statute in a reserve for distribution under either a fixed price sale (with the price set at $1,500 per ton) and an allowance auction.[9]

The acid rain programme is being implemented through regulations being promulgated by the Environmental Protection Agency. Its success in lowering the cost of reducing acid rain pollutants will depend on these regulations as well as on the actions of electric utilities, state Public Utility Commissions and others (see Wile 1991). Studies sponsored by the Environmental Protection Agency predict that the trading approach can reduce utility compliance cost by as much as 20 to 50 percent compared to the traditional regulatory approach. The cost savings could be even greater if industrial sources decide to opt into the trading programme.

Other initiatives

The 1990 Clean Air Act contained several initiatives other than the acid rain trading programme. These include mandatory as well as discretionary economic incentive programmes (Elman et al. 1992). For example, any state may choose to adopt an emissions trading programme as part of its State Implementation Plan to demonstrate compliance with federal ambient standards. Trading can also apply to mobile sources through options for refiners and others to participate in emission credit programmes—much like the earlier lead trading programme——for reformulated gasoline or oxygenated gasoline.

The eventual scope of emissions trading in the United States will depend in large part on the initiative that states and local air quality agencies take to implement the increased flexibility called for in the 1990 Clean Air Act. The state of California has developed a number of emissions trading initiatives (see Harrison and Nichols 1990c). These include most prominently the emissions trading programme being developed for the Los Angeles Air Basin by the South Coast Air Quality Management District (see the Appendix for a detailed description of this programme) and various mobile source emissions trading programmes being developed by the California Air Resources Board.

b) Other experience and proposals

The United States is not alone in its interest in emissions trading. Germany has used a limited form of emissions trading for several years (see Tietenberg 1992). Under this programme, plants are allowed to obtain offsets to construct new plants in areas above ambient air quality standards; this programme is similar to the offset programme developed in the United States. Plants are also allowed to develop alternative emission reduction programmes for new plants if they can demonstrate that they achieve the same results. In contrast to the netting programme in the United States, the German programme does not limit the offsetting reductions to the same pollutant.

Several other countries are developing serious proposals for emissions trading to deal with key environmental problems. In Canada, emissions trading proposals have been developed for stationary sources of nitrogen oxides in Ontario (see Nichols and Harrison 1990a and Nichols 1992) and for sulphur dioxide and greenhouse gases in Alberta (see Nichols and Harrison 1991 and Nichols 1992). These proposals have been sponsored both by individual provinces and by the Canadian

Council of Ministers of the Environment, which has also released a policy framework for designing emissions trading programmes (Canadian Council of Ministers of the Environment 1991).

Proposals for emissions trading have also been developed in other countries, including China, the United Kingdom, and Poland (see Tietenberg 1992). Although the details remain sketchy and their prospects for adoption are uncertain, the fact that emissions trading programmes are being discussed indicates their growing importance in international environmental policy.

In addition to these national programmes, there has been considerable discussion of an international emissions trading programme to deal with global warming. Both the OECD and the United Nations have recently published reports on the topic (OECD 1992b and United Nations Conference on Trade and Development 1992). In addition, officials in the United States in 1990 proposed an emissions trading approach for controlling global warming that would be implemented on an international basis (see Stewart 1990 and Schmalensee 1990).

3. Summary and implications

The overall conclusion from reviewing experience and commentary on economic instruments—particularly recent developments—is that both emissions taxes and emissions trading proposals are likely to become increasingly important in future environmental policy. Such policies fit in with general objectives of harnessing markets and using economic incentives to promote social goals. The list of potential new programmes ranges from very localized taxes—such as a tax on municipal solid waste—to international taxes or trading systems for global pollutants.

Determining which of these various tax or trading proposals are likely to be implemented and which programmes are likely to become significant would be major undertakings.[10] Many factors will enter into the choice of public policy in this area, including the importance of cost savings, the compatibility of economic instruments with administrative and institutional structures, and political acceptability (Barde 1991). In any event, it seems likely that the increased public attention regarding economic instruments will expand the need for careful analyses of these proposals, including analyses of their distributive implications for key sectors and groups.

Chapter 3

Framework for Assessing the Distributive
Implications of Economic Instruments

All policies have distributive implications. Some individuals gain. Others may lose. It is much more difficult to generalize about these *individual* gains and losses than about the *overall* efficiency impacts. Economic theory shows that overall costs are reduced with economic instruments; no such theory informs the pattern of individual gains and losses. Nevertheless, it is possible to provide a conceptual foundation to structure an empirical study.

Establishing the *nature* of the distributive analysis is the first task for a systematic treatment of distributive impacts. This chapter therefore discusses several threshold questions designed to clarify the distributive analysis. This discussion provides a structure for assessing distributive effects of economic instruments. The following chapter builds on this structure and traditional microeconomic principles to provide a *conceptual* analysis of distributional impacts.

A. Threshold issues for a distributive analysis

The following are threshold issues that should be considered in structuring a distributive analysis of an economic instrument. Although some of these same issues apply to an efficiency analysis, they apply with greater force here because there are many more options and less agreement on what should be covered.

1. Against what baseline should the distributive impacts of economic instruments be measured?

2. Will the economic instrument result in government revenues?

3. How can initial incidence be distinguished from final incidence?

4. Within what time frame should distributive impacts be measured?

5. For what groups should distributive impacts be assessed?

6. What modelling technique should be used to assess distributive impacts?

1. Benchmark for comparison to economic instruments

This is perhaps the key threshold issue. There are two polar benchmark cases: (1) the status quo with *no* environmental regulation in place; or (2) an equivalent command-and-control programme. For example, one could compare the impacts of the United States acid rain trading programme either to no federal controls on SO_2 emissions from existing power plants or to hypothetical command-and-control regulations that would achieve the same reduction in SO_2 emissions.

There is no hard and fast rule about which benchmark is correct. In some cases it is sensible to compare economic incentives to the "no regulation" case. Completely new environmental taxes or trading programmes without any regulatory alternatives are likely to be judged—at least by those harmed—in comparison to the status quo rather than in comparison with what *might* be done. However, in cases in which economic incentives are supplanting regulation or in which both approaches are being evaluated, it seems more useful to evaluate economic incentives in comparison to an alternative approach. That is, after all, how we typically evaluate the overall efficiency gains. One usually does not ask whether an emissions tax or trading scheme would reduce costs—or improve efficiency—relative to "no regulation" but rather relative to the alternative regulatory approach.

Deciding to take a comparative approach carries three implications. First, one must identify the *alternative regulatory approach*. In the case of the United States acid rain trading programme, for example, one would have to identify the set of emission standards that would yield the same total reduction in sulphur dioxide as projected under the trading programme.

A second implication of the comparative approach is that the *benefits* of environmental controls would *not* be part of the analysis. If the same total level of emissions is achieved with both types of regulations, both the overall level of benefits and their distributive effects would not differ.[11] In contrast, if an environmental tax or trading programme were judged relative to the unregulated status quo, the distributive effects of the benefits would be an important element of the overall impact.[12]

The third implication of the comparative approach is that the distributional impacts are not a zero-sum-game. Society as a whole stands to gain from introducing economic incentives. In general, we would expect these gains to be shared among various groups, although, as noted below, some groups could lose.

2. Revenue collection

The economic instruments considered in this study—emission tax and trading schemes—are generally very similar. Both instruments tend to reduce the overall costs of meeting environmental targets. Both provide incentives for technological progress. Both tend to decentralize decision-making and shift the administrative burdens of rule making from pollution control agencies to polluters.

The distributive impacts of the instruments, however, differ considerably depending upon whether or not the government collects revenues. As noted above, these revenues are *transfers* from an overall societal standpoint and do not represent real resource costs to society. Any revenue the government collects from an emissions tax or from the initial sale of allowances will go to reduce other taxes or pay for other government expenditures. However, these changes *do* affect the distributive effects. Changes from one tax regime to another will affect some groups more than others. Spending the added revenues will similarly mean gains to some groups and costs the others. The point is simply that distributive analyses require a more complex analyses than is typically performed to judge the efficiency of economic instruments.[13]

For this element of the analysis, the key distinction is not between taxes and allowances but rather between schemes that raise government revenues and those that do not. The following two "types" of economic instruments are distinguished:

1. *Taxes and auctioned allowances.* Both taxes and auctioned allowances generate government revenues.

2. *"Grandfathered" allowances.* Emission allowances are allocated "free of charge" to firms in the first instance.

The precise distributive impacts will of course depend upon the details of one or another of these two types.[14] How high is the tax? How many allowances are auctioned? What is the formula for allocating allowances under the "grandfathered" alternative? But there is a threshold issue concerning which of these two basic types is involved and thus what initial burdens are created by the policy.

3. Initial incidence versus final incidence

Increased tax revenues and changes in business costs are key elements of the *initial* incidence of a programme. That is, initially, businesses will face higher costs from new regulatory requirements (or lower costs under the comparative approach). But this initial cost incidence does not answer the question of final incidence: On whom, ultimately, does the effect of the policy fall?

To answer this question requires looking beyond the initial effects. There are two basic principles involved.[15] First, eventually, all costs and benefits are borne by individuals. Although costs may initially be paid by business firms, their ultimate burden must be traced to individual households in their capacities as owners of the firms, as employees, as owners of other (non-labour) factors of production, or as consumers of the products. Second, the ultimate burdens and benefits may differ quite considerably from the initial effects. Firms and individuals make adjustments that have the effect of shifting the burden or benefit.

The conceptual analysis in the following chapter explains the circumstances in which businesses can shift costs to consumers. Faced with higher costs for pollution control expenditures or emissions taxes, businesses will raise their prices, hoping to pass the burden of the tax to buyers. Buyers in turn will attempt to avoid the higher prices by shifting their purchases to other products. The ultimate outcome will depend upon these various responses. The key point here is that the resulting chain of adjustments—the process of "shifting the cost burden"—may lead to a final or *ultimate* incidence which differs greatly from the initial incidence.

Although the need to consider "shifting" is clearest in the case of cost, the same process can occur for the benefits of environmental improvement. Consider the case of improvements in urban air quality. The benefits accrue initially to households living in the areas whose air quality has improved. But landlords may attempt to obtain some of these benefits by raising rents. Renters will respond by considering moving to other, now less expensive, neighbourhoods. The ultimate impacts will depend upon demand and supply conditions in the housing market. Again, the key point is that shifting can lead to an ultimate incidence of benefits that differs substantially from the initial situation.

4. Timing of impacts and "transition costs"

A related issue concerns the timing of the impacts to be considered. Most economic analyses focus on the *long-term* impacts of regulatory requirements on producer costs and market prices. Like the tax incidence analyses that they resemble, analyses of the distributional impacts of regulatory requirements typically estimate the increased burdens on firms or households after adjustment to a new set of equilibrium quantities and prices.

Such a long-run analysis ignores the costs that accrue to individuals and groups during the *transition*—the adjustment from one regulatory state to another. (See Baumol and Oates 1988 and Harrison 1981 for discussions of transitional costs.) As Baumol and Oates observe, whether environmental improvements are achieved by economic instruments or by direct regulation, the effects will hit some industries much harder than others. If regulations are strengthened, heavy polluters may be lead to curtail operations significantly and perhaps even close down altogether. This means that one of the most significant transitional costs from environmental programmes will be a loss of jobs.

Conventional long-term, comparative-static analyses ignore these transitional costs on the assumption that they have no lasting impact: following a temporary period of unemployment, full employment is reestablished. The long-term incidence then depends upon changes in the equilibrium set of prices and output.

But these transitional costs figure very prominently in the public debate surrounding policy changes—including those involving environmental issues—both at the national and international levels. Many believe that the transition of human and other resources to new uses following a policy shift will impose losses on workers in particular localities or particular industries.

Should these transitional impacts be considered in assessing the distributive impacts of economic instruments? Although there is an argument to be made that these impacts can be overstated—as workers threatened with layoffs fail to see the new options they will have—it seems clear that transitional impacts *should* be included in a complete analysis. It is important to clarify how jobs are likely to be affected by economic incentive schemes and what (if anything) should be done to mitigate losses.

5. Groupings for distributive impacts

The issue of transition costs and job impacts raises another threshold issue: for what groups should distributional impacts be assessed? As noted, it is traditional to focus on the impacts on different income groups. Indeed, the two concepts are often used interchangeably. The focus on whether costs are regressive (more burdensome to the poor) or progressive (more burdensome to the rich) is due in part to a long tradition of analysing the incidence of taxes. The costs of environmental regulation share many of the conceptual properties of taxes and thus their distributive impacts can be evaluated using the same basic formulation.

There are in fact many groupings of individuals that might be of interest in a distributive analysis, not just income groups, particularly if one considers the transitional costs as well as the long-term costs of programmes. The possible groups include the following:

- producers as a group;

- consumers as a group;

- taxpayers as a group;

- specific groups of producers (e.g., specific industries, big firms versus small firms, high-cost versus low-cost, industrialized country versus developing country, etc.);

- employees and other suppliers of services or materials to producers whose output is affected by environmental regulation;

- specific groups of households in their capacities as consumers, shareholders, taxpayers or employees (e.g., low income versus high income, industrialized country versus developing country, etc.); and

- people in different generations.

As noted above, it is important to emphasize that eventually all costs are borne by households. The public discussion is often muddled by claims that "business should pay for environmental programmes"—or by the assumption that business *does* pay for the programmes—not appreciating that "business costs" eventually accrue to individuals. In that regard, some of the groups mentioned above can be misleading. For example, "small firms" does not necessarily mean "low income," because small businesses may be owned by wealthy individuals.

Which groups should be the focus of concern? There is no "right" answer and certainly the choice may well depend on the specific policy issue at stake. But there appear to be strong reasons to go beyond economists' traditional focus on income distributional impacts to include other groups, if for no other reason than that estimating income impacts requires intermediate analyses of impacts on producers, consumers and employees. Moreover, many discussions of equity in connection with environmental rules are concerned more with some notion of "fairness" than with income distribution.

6. Analytical tools

A sixth and final threshold issue concerns the analytic tool that will be used to assess distributive impacts. This is a threshold issue because the modelling tool will influence the range of impacts that can be estimated. There are a host of possibilities ranging from "back-of-the envelope" calculations to complex general equilibrium models that simulate the workings of entire national (or even international) economic systems. (See Denny and Smith 1991 for a review of various modelling options). Among the options that have been used to assess distributive impacts in the past are the following:

1. *Partial equilibrium impact assessment.* This is the most common approach for relatively simple cases. Data on changes in business costs are used to assess changes in prices of key products. Expenditure patterns are used to distribute the price increases to different groups (e.g., income groups).

2. *Input-output model.* This is the simplest class of models that take into account interactions of various elements of the economy. The "fixed coefficient" assumption means that these models are most useful for short-term analysis.

3. *Macroeconomic model.* More detailed macroeconomic models can be used to model the many interactions among various sectors (factor markets, product markets) that determine the effects of using economic instruments. These models can be used for short-term and longer-term analyses to assess the results "with" and "without" the economic instrument in place.

4. *Computable general equilibrium model.* These models are specifically designed to investigate the long-run process of economic adjustments to policy changes, by examining how relative prices of all goods and factors of production would have to adjust to achieve equilibrium in all markets.

The appropriate model will depend upon the nature of the economic instrument as well as on the budget for analysis. The majority of distributive analyses are based upon the relatively simple partial equilibrium approach, which is sensible for policies whose impacts tend to be focused on a relatively narrow segment of the economy. The methodological discussion in the next chapter concentrates on this approach. However, the alternative methodologies are discussed in the context of empirical analyses of the carbon tax.

B. Structure of a distributive analysis

The discussion of threshold issues emphasized that there is no *one* format for a distributive analysis. Figure 3 provides a summary of the initial impacts based upon alternative assumptions regarding the following two key choices:

1. The benchmark against which impacts are evaluated.

2. Whether or not the economic instrument involves the collection of government revenues.

The initial impacts in Figure 3 relate to a long-term distributive analysis.

Consider the entries in the fourth column as an example of the way in which these assumptions structure the analysis. The fourth column entries show the qualitative results we would expect for an emissions trading programme in which the benchmark is a command-and-control regulatory regime that achieves the same environmental improvement and in which allowances are grandfathered in the first instance. This is the case that applies to the acid rain trading programme contained in the United States 1990 Clean Air Act. The initial (pre-shifting) impacts would be positive. Business as a whole would see lower costs initially: control costs decline and the government does not collect tax revenues. Households would typically be unaffected initially, since environmental benefits would be the same. (If households were included in the programme—for example through programmes aimed at automotive operation—the initial impacts would be positive since costs would be lower under the economic incentive programme.) Government revenues would be unchanged and administrative costs would, if anything, decrease.

This case can be contrasted with that in the first column in which the benchmark is no regulation and in which a tax or auctioned allowance approach is used. A long-run analysis would take as its starting point *increases* in the costs to business both for control costs and for payments to governments for taxes or initial allowance purchases. (As a group, businesses do not receive trading revenues when allowances are auctioned.) Households would initially receive benefits and may initially bear costs if they are included in the programme. Governments of course would receive increased revenues but would also face increased administrative costs. The long-run analysis of this case is therefore very different than that in the fourth column.

What lessons are learned from this taxonomy? Perhaps the basic lesson is that the first step in assessing the distributive effects of an economic instrument programme is to be clear about what is at stake. Different assumptions regarding the nature of the baseline and nature of the economic incentive mechanism can lead to very different analyses.

Figure 4. **Initial impacts of economic instruments under alternative assumptions**

Sector	No Regulation		"Command and Control"	
	Taxes/Auctioned Allowances	Grandfathered Allowances	Taxes/Auctioned Allowances	Grandfathered Allowances
	(1)	(2)	(3)	(4)
Business				
Control Costs	Increase	Increase	Decrease	Decrease
Tax/Allowance Payments	Increase	None	Increase	None
Government				
Tax/Allowance Revenues	Increase	None	Increase	None
Administrative Costs	Increase	Increase	Decrease (?)	Decrease (?)
Households				
Environment Benefits	Increase	Increase	None	None
Control Costs	Increase	Increase	Decrease	Decrease

Regulatory Benchmark

Chapter 4

Conceptual Analyses of the Distributive Impacts of Economic Instruments

In this chapter the tools of microeconomic analysis are used to provide a conceptual framework for estimating the distributive impacts of economic instruments on different groups. This chapter first considers the long-term impacts of economic instruments, which is the perspective of most distributive studies. The chapter then considers the additional issues that arise in estimating the impacts of economic instruments during a transition from one regulatory regime to another. The chapter concludes with a summary of the key steps in estimating distributive impacts.

A. Analyses of long-term impacts

This section describes the steps involved in analysing the long-run impacts of economic instruments on various groups in society.[16] The relatively simple case is presented first, in which costs or benefits are initially borne by households, and then the much more complex case is considered, in which costs are initially borne by business firms.

1. Initial impacts on households

The first step would be to identify costs or benefits that are initially borne by households. As noted in the previous chapter, households would initially bear costs if they were included in the economic incentive programme. The most prominent example of a programme that would target households initially is an automotive emission tax that would be paid directly by individuals (see White 1982).

If households had to pay an emissions tax or participate in an emissions trading programme based upon the emissions from their automobiles, they would face higher costs for operating their vehicles. Estimating these initial costs would constitute the first step in the empirical analysis. If a comparative approach were used, this step would include estimates of the initial costs due to an equivalent command-and-control strategy.

If a "no regulation" benchmark were used in the distributive analysis, it would be necessary to estimate the size of the environmental gains as well. For example, reductions in automotive emissions due to a tax or trading policy would translate into reductions in air quality, which in turn could be used to estimate health and welfare benefits.[17] The result of this analysis would be estimates of the dollar costs and dollar benefits initially borne by individuals under an economic incentive strategy.

2. Incidence of household costs and environmental benefits on various groups

Determining the final incidence is quite straightforward for costs and benefits that accrue initially to households. For example, a programme targeted on automotive emissions might raise automotive operating costs and improve air quality in various regions. Information on the relative automotive expenditures by households in different income groups can be used to determine the income distribution pattern of these costs. Households would avoid part of the potential costs because of their reactions to price changes. Thus, the analysis would include an assessment of the price elasticity of demand and the resulting changes vehicle ownership and use. Such an analysis would be equivalent to that done to determine the impact of an increase in excise taxes on automobiles or fuel. (See Lambert 1989 for a theoretical treatment and Harrison 1974 for an example of a distributive study of automotive emissions controls.)

Determining the distribution of environmental benefits would involve obtaining information on the average changes in pollutant exposure for households in different groups. Such an analysis would allow one to assess the average physical changes that accrue to households in different income groups. There are, however, two conceptual complications in assessing the final distribution of environmental benefits:

- *Differences in valuation.* Households in different income (or other) groups may differ in the dollar value they place on environmental improvements; and

- *Benefit shifting from renters to owners.* As noted above, the gains may be shifted to owners if housing prices increase when air quality is improved.

In theory, it would be possible to obtain information on both of these factors. For example, housing price studies have evaluated both differences in valuation across income groups and the possibility that air quality benefits are shifted to owners (see Harrison and Rubinfeld 1978b).

3. Overview of issues regarding the incidence of business costs

Most environmental regulations are designed to control emissions from industrial sources, such as factories and power plants. Thus the initial costs of most programmes will fall on business. That means that firms initially gain the cost savings advantages from reductions in costs due to economic instruments, or bear the cost increases. The ultimate incidence of these costs (or cost savings) on households will depend upon how much of the changes are passed through to customers in the form of changes in product prices, and how much stay with the owners of firms in the form of changes in profits. (There may be changes in other markets, such as changes in wage rates or land prices; but these are generally understood to be second-order effects compared to the changes in prices and business profits.)

After the price changes are estimated, the distributional impacts can be calculated by determining the role of various products in the expenditure patterns of households in the relevant groups. To calculate the costs or gains for households in different income groups, for example, one would use information on the price increases and the role of the goods whose prices had changed in their expenditure patterns. This analysis is equivalent to the distributive analysis of various excise taxes. Price changes for "necessities"—that is, goods whose consumption does not change greatly with higher income—would tend to be regressive. Price changes for luxury goods bought by the wealthy would tend to be progressive.

The portion of the cost change that stays with business firms would also have distributive impacts. Corporate profits tend to accrue to wealthy individuals, and thus any changes in profits will be progressive. However, corporate profits tend to be shared between owners and the government because of the tax on corporate profits. Thus, the ultimate incidence for changes in corporate profits would depend upon the income pattern of federal taxpayers, which is much less progressive. The net effect is an empirical proposition. (See Harrison 1974 for an example of such an empirical study.)

The calculations for business costs are thus similar to those outlined above for programmes aimed directly at household purchases, except for the preliminary steps of estimating changes in business costs. As discussed below, determining the changes in business costs can be complicated since it depends upon the specific elements of the emission tax or trading programme. The conceptual discussion in this section is divided into three separate issues:

- the size of the *initial* costs that accrue to various firms affected by emissions tax or trading programmes;

- the *final* incidence of these costs on business stockholders and customers due to price changes; and

- the influence of the "opportunity cost" of grandfathered emission allowances on product prices and therefore the *revised* impacts on customers.

These three issues are discussed in turn.

4. Initial impacts of economic instruments on business costs

The simple example given in Chapter 2 illustrated how compliance costs *decrease* relative to a command-and-control system under emissions trading and emissions taxes. It is useful to provide a more detailed treatment of the costs to firms under different economic instruments. The following analyses show:

- how control costs decline under trading with grandfathered allowances;

- how important the allocation formula is in determining gains and losses; and

- how most firms will face cost increases under auctioned allowances or emissions taxes.

a) Compliance cost savings to high-cost and low-cost firms with trading

Each plant's marginal cost of controlling emissions can be thought of as its demand curve for emissions allowances; the maximum amount that a firm is willing to pay for another ton of emissions is equal to what it would save from controlling one ton less. Figure 4 plots hypothetical demand curves for the two plants included in the example in Chapter 2. Plant I is the low cost plant and Plant II is the high cost plant. Note that the horizontal axis measures the number of tons *emitted*; i.e., as *emissions decrease*, the amount of *control increases*. Because the marginal costs tend to increase as controls become more stringent, the demand curve rises as emissions decline.

The graph assumes that the benchmark emission standard would require that each plant reduce its emissions to 100 tons. In the absence of regulation, the plants would emit to the point where their marginal control costs were zero. Thus, the shaded areas show the *total* cost to each plant of the standard. The *marginal* cost of the standard is, as in the simple example given, $500 per ton for Plant I and $3,000 per ton for Plant II.

Figure 5. **Firms' demand curves for emissions allowances**

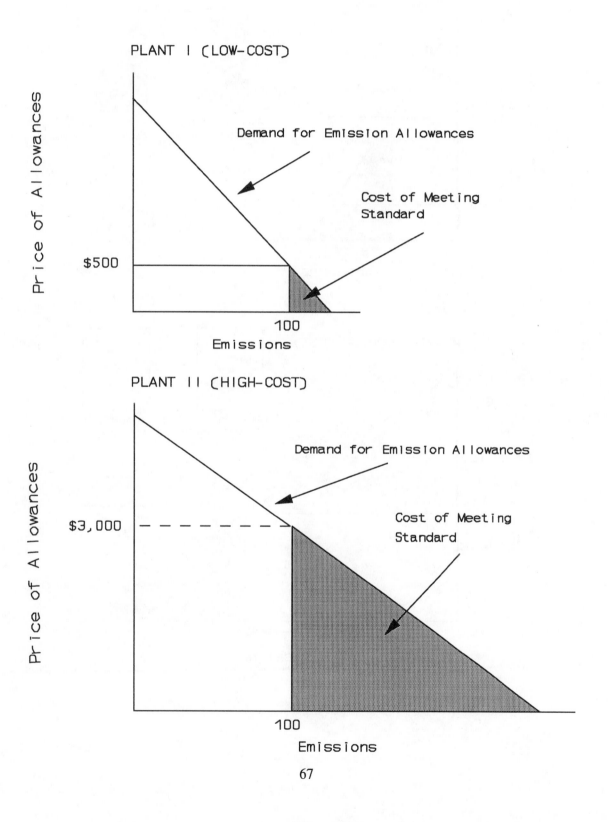

Figure 6. Cost savings to firms from emissions trading

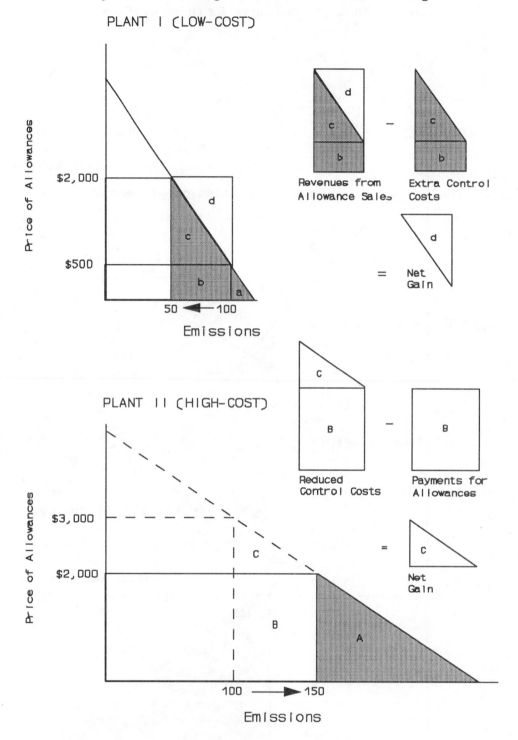

? shows the savings from trading. (Table II shows the various components of costs in tabular form.) Plant I (the lower-cost one) incurs additional control costs as it reduces its emissions from 100 to 50; those extra costs are shown by the shaded trapezoid *(b+c)*, the area of which is $62,500. That extra cost is more than offset, however, by revenues from the 50 allowances that it sells to Plant II at $2,000 each, as shown by the rectangle *(b+c+d)*, the area of which is $100,000. Thus, the net gain to Plant I is the area of the triangle *(d)*, which is $37,500.

The lower half of the figure shows the results for Plant II, which increases its emissions from 100 to 150 tons. It reduces control costs by the area of the trapezoid *(B+C)*, which has a value of $125,000. That gain is partly offset by the cost of purchasing 50 allowances from Plant I, which, at a cost of $2,000 each, equals $100,000 (the area of the rectangle *B*). Thus, the net savings to Plant II is $25,000; combined with Plant I's savings of $37,500, the overall gain for the two plants is $62,500. From the perspective of the rest of society, emissions are unchanged, and there has been no cost to the government, so the net overall gain is also $62,500.

b) *Factors affecting cost savings*

These figures show that relative to uniform standards, the options under economic instruments lead to savings in compliance costs for all firms. There are three factors that influence the size of the cost savings a given firm will experience:

1. *Marginal cost relative to the allowance price.* Both low-cost and high-cost firms will share in the gains under the trading programme. The only firms that will not gain are those that do not trade, presumably because the standard is "right" for them; i.e., the prevailing price of allowances is equal to their marginal cost of control at the standard. This observation points out that although no firms incur higher costs, the gains from the trading programme may differ widely, with the greatest gains going to the two extremes (lowest and highest-cost compliers).

2. *Level of allowance price.* The size of the gains to individual firms or industries depends upon the price level. Net sellers gain more the greater the allowance price. Net buyers gain less the higher the allowance price. The price will be determined by the cumulative demand for allowances among all participants. That demand depends upon the control options that are available. As control options become more expensive, given the level of overall allowances, the price of allowances will tend to increase. Conversely, if control costs decline, the allowance price will tend to decrease. The number of participants also will influence the price for emissions allowances. More participants do not necessarily mean a higher price. Whether the price increases or decreases depends upon the new participants' control costs relative to the additional emissions allocations they introduce into the system.

3. *Allocation of allowances.* Our example assumes that allowances are allocated under trading in precisely the same way as with the command-and-control alternative. That is, we assume that each of the firms in our simple example would have been allowed to emit 100 tons per year.[18] The allocation of allowances generally does *not* affect the potential for overall cost savings from trading. But it does affect the distribution

of gains among the participants in the programme. Indeed, this issue of the allocation of allowances is critical to an understanding of the impacts of a trading programme on individual firms.

c) Changing the allocation of allowances

? shows the impact of changing the allocation of allowances so that Plant I gets 70 tons (30 fewer than under the standards) and Plant II gets 130 tons (30 more). (Table II also shows the components of costs under this alternative allocation formula.) Changing the allocation does not affect the allowance price. The distribution of costs, however, is considerably different when initial allocations of allowances are changed.

Figure 7. Impacts of alternative allowance allocations on firm costs

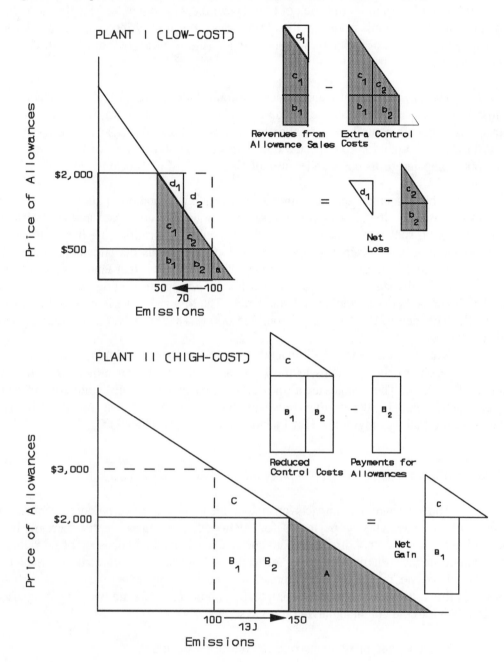

For Plant I, the low-cost firm, reducing the number of allowances leads to costs with trading that are *higher* than under the standard. As with the case of an allocation equal to the standard, Plant I pays more (the area of the trapezoid $c_1+c_2+b_1+b_2$, or \$62,500) to reduce emissions by an additional 50 tons, from 100 tons to 50 tons. But it only receives payments for 20 of those tons (*area $d_1+c_1+b_1$*), or a total of \$40,000. As a result, its total costs are \$22,500 higher than under the standard.

The losses to Plant I are reflected in *additional* gains to Plant II. Plant II receives 130 tons, 30 tons more than under the standard. Relative to the standard, it increases emissions by 50 tons, thus reducing control costs by the area of the trapezoid B_1+B_2+C, for a savings of \$125,000. But it only has to pay for 20 tons, at a total cost of \$40,000 (the area of B_2). Thus, overall it gains \$85,000 compared to its costs under an emission standard of 100 tons.

Table II summarizes the results of changing the allocation of allowances. The first column shows results when the allocation is the same as under the command-and-control approach. The second column shows the results of the changed initial allocation. Reducing Plant I's allocation reduces its allowance receipts by \$60,000. This figure equals the allowance price (\$2,000) times the reduction in the initial allocation (30 tons). The net result is that Plant I pays \$25,000 more than it would under the standard. Note that this loss is *not* due to trading but rather to the change in initial allocation between trading and standards. The loss to Plant I is reflected in an added gain to Plant II. The gain to Plant II jumps from \$25,000 to \$85,000 when it receives 30 additional tons of allowances.

Note that the change in impacts is due to the change in initial allocation does *not* affect the final results or the net gains to the firms as a whole. Under either case, the net gain from trading is \$62,500. The changes are a transfer—one party's loss is just counterbalanced by another's gain. From Plant I's perspective, however, the loss is a real cost and the firm is unlikely to welcome the trading programme if it included the changed allocation.

d) *Effect of emissions taxes or auctioning allowances on firms' costs*

The distributional impacts change a great deal if government revenues are involved. Emissions tax payments or payments for auctioned allowances clearly increase business costs, assuming that they are not directly rebated or "recycled" back. (The issue of recycling government revenue to reduce distributional—or efficiency—impacts is discussed in Chapter 6.) If the benchmark is "no regulation," government revenues simply add to the costs initially borne by business firms. However, under the comparative approach, there are two offsetting effects on firms costs relative to the command-and-control system:

- economic instruments *reduce* control costs; and

- payments for taxes or auctioned allowances *increase* costs. Which of these two effects dominates will depend upon the details of the programmes.

? illustrates the impacts of adding either an emissions tax or auctioned allowances on both the high-cost and low-cost firms. The levels of emissions for both plants would be identical to the case of grandfathered allowances. If the emissions tax were set at \$2,000 per ton, Plant I would

Table II. **Summary of trading gains and losses under alternative allowance allocations**

	Numerical Example	
	Same Allocation as Command-and-Control	Changed Allocation
Plant I (low cost)		
Initial Allocation	100 tons	70 tons
Change in Control Cost	-$62,500	-$62,500
Allowance Receipts	100,000	40,000
Net Change	$37,500	-$22,500
Plant II (high cost)		
Initial Allocation	100 tons	130 tons
Change in Control Cost	$125,000	$125,000
Allowance Payments	-100,000	-40,000
Net Change	$25,000	$85,000
Overall		
Total Allowances	200 tons	200 tons
Net Gain	$62,500	$62,500

Source: Illustrative calculations as explained in text.

reduce its emissions from 100 to 50. Similarly, Plant II would increase its emissions from 100 to 150. Both firms would adjust their control levels to the point that their marginal control costs equalled the tax, just as in the earlier cases.

The distributive impacts are much different, however. For Plant I, the low-cost firm, the impact of an emission tax or trading with an auction is clearly negative; first, it pays $62,500 (the trapezoid b+c) to reduce emissions from 100 to 50 tons. In addition, it must pay taxes or buy allowances at the government auction on the 50 tons that remain, at a cost of $2,000 each, for a total of $100,000 (the area of the rectangle e+f). As a result, its total cost is $162,500 higher than under the standard.

The situation facing Plant II (the high-cost firm) is more complicated, involving the tradeoff noted above. It increases its emissions and thus reduces its control costs by the area of the trapezoid (B+C), resulting in a saving of $125,000. But it must pay taxes on a total of 150 tons of emissions (or buy at auction 150 allowances), at a cost of $300,000. Thus, overall its net costs increase by $175,000 compared to the emission standard of 100 tons.

High-cost firms could come out ahead under some circumstances. If the cost savings from reducing control are great enough (the net effect of cost savings and tax payments is equal to the area of the triangle C), they will exceed the cost of having to pay taxes or buy allowances to cover emissions allowed free under the standard.

Table III summarizes the illustrative results for emissions taxes or auctioned allowances. Relative to grandfathered allowances, the tax/auction approach costs the two plants $400,000 ($62,500 + $337,500). The firms must pay taxes or buy allowances for a total of 200 tons at a cost of $2,000 each, rather than emit them free of charge. Of course, this $400,000 is *not* a net cost to society, but rather a transfer from these firms (initially at least) to the government treasury. That is, the loss to the firms is just counterbalanced by a gain to the treasury.

Figure 8. **Impacts of emissions taxes or auctioned allowances on firm costs**

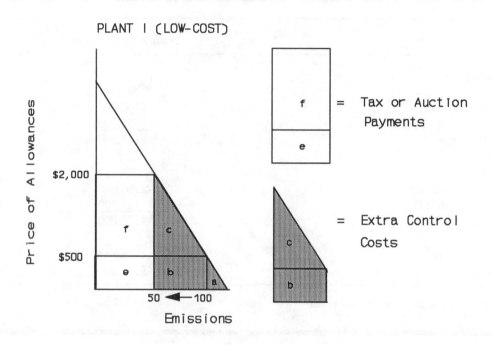

PLANT I (LOW-COST)

Price of Allowances

$2,000

$500

50 ◄── 100

Emissions

f = Tax or Auction
Payments
e

c = Extra Control
b   Costs

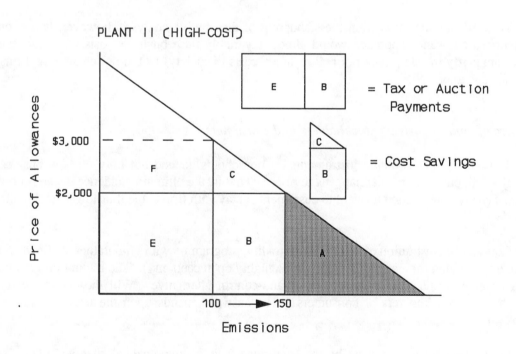

PLANT II (HIGH-COST)

Price of Allowances

$3,000

$2,000

100 ──► 150

Emissions

E | B = Tax or Auction
Payments

c
B = Cost Savings

Table III. **Summary of trading gains and losses under the tax or auction approach**

	Numerical Example
Plant I (low cost)	
Emissions	50 tons
Cost of Tax/Auction	-$100,000
Increased Control Cost	- 62,500
Net Change	-$162,500
Plant II (high cost)	
Emissions	150 tons
Cost of Tax/Auction	-$300,000
Reduced Control Cost	125,000
Net Change	-$175,000
Overall	
Total Emissions	200 tons
Net Gain	-$337,500

Source: Illustrative calculations as explained in text.

The critical conclusion from the standpoint of distributive analyses, however, is that the tax or auctioned allowance approach would almost invariably raise business costs. The fact that these costs are partly transfers (and not real resource costs to society) would not change the firms' antipathy for this approach.

5. *Incidence of control costs on stockholders and consumers*

The impacts of economic instruments on households depend not only on how business costs are affected, but also on what happens to prices. That is, the ultimate incidence depends upon whether cost changes are shifted forward to customers or stay with firms (and thus lower stockholder profits).

Consider the institution of an emissions trading programme with grandfathered allowances in a single urban region (or a single country with a highly open economy). The trading programme results in lower costs relative to the command-and-control alternative. Will those cost savings accrue to business stockholders or consumers? The answer depends upon the nature of market conditions.

One polar case is illustrated by the conditions facing a hypothetical chemical plant that operates in national (or international) markets. Figure 8 shows its market conditions. The supply curve S_0 represents the initial condition under command-and-control. The supply curve slopes up (firms will supply more if the price rises), representing the firms' marginal cost of production, i.e., how much it costs to produce another unit of production. Because the firm operates in national (or international) markets, its output is too small to have any noticeable effect on the prices of its products. Thus, the demand curve facing the chemical plant is flat; the price does not change regardless of how much the firm produces. Under the command-and-control cost conditions, the equilibrium output is Q_0. With the cost savings from trading, the supply curve shifts out to S_1, leading to a new equilibrium at Q_1. There is no pressure to lower prices because they are set by national or international forces of supply and demand, and these forces would not be affected by a cost decrease limited to a single urban region. The price does not change. Thus, with national industries, the cost savings translate into increased gains to firms. (Workers may also gain from the increase in demand for their services that would follow from chemical manufacturers decisions to expand output in the region.)

Figure 9. Cost savings under emissions trading for national industries accrue to stockholders

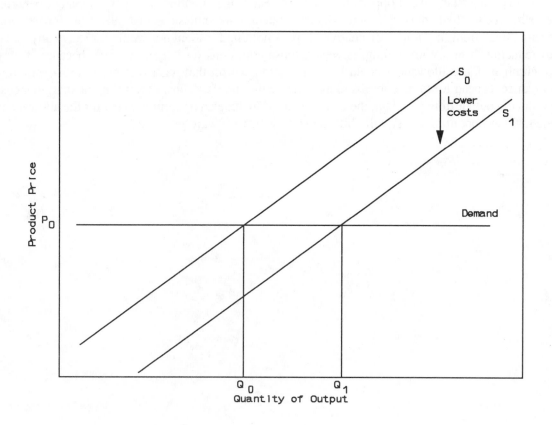

The opposite case is illustrated by the situation that would face dry cleaners within a given region. A dry cleaning firm may compete with several nearby firms, but all of them would be within the urban region. If emissions trading lead to lower costs, those lower costs would tend to be translated into lower prices for dry cleaning services. Figure 9 shows the impacts of cost reductions for "local" industries; i.e., those markets for which local supply is an important determinant of price. In such industries, both consumers and stockholders would gain from the cost savings due to emissions trading. The size of the gains to stockholders or consumers depends upon the relative size of the demand and supply elasticities.[19]

6. Potential offsetting impacts from opportunity cost of allowances

This generally positive set of impacts on consumers from reduced cost must be tempered by the fact that emissions trading means that firms must consider the "opportunity cost" of emissions in a manner that they do not with typical standards. These opportunity costs will tend to at least partly offset the impacts of lower costs.

To understand these opportunity costs, consider the situation facing a company operating an existing facility that emits pollution. Under a standard, the emissions that fall within the existing rules are "free" from the firm's perspective. It pays nothing for them nor would it receive any value from reducing them. With trading, however, those emissions no longer are free, because if they were eliminated, the allowances could be sold to another firm that wished to expand its operations or to reduce its need for more controls to meet tightening limits. Thus, in figuring the marginal cost of producing output from the plant, the company must include an opportunity cost for the allowances needed. That opportunity cost will shift the supply curve inward.

Figure 10. **Cost savings under emissions trading for local industries are shared by stockholders and consumers**

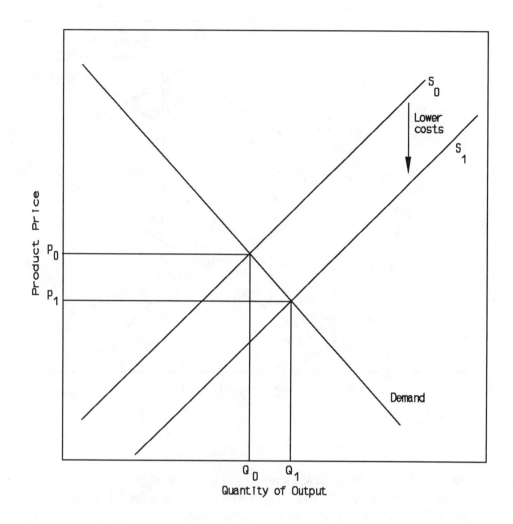

Figure 11. **The net impact under emissions trading on prices depends on the size of opportunity costs of allowances relative to cost savings**

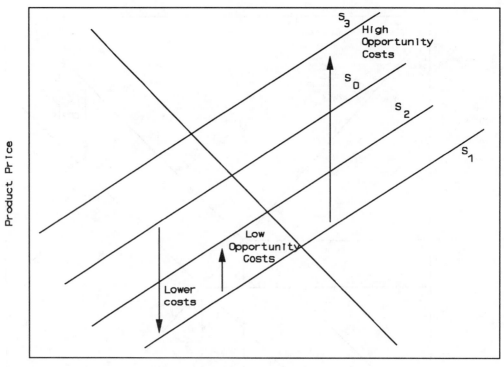

? illustrates this effect for a local industry. As before in Figure 8, the supply curve with standards is S_0, while the impact of the cost savings with trading is reflected in the curve S_1. If the opportunity cost of the allowances is less than the cost savings—as shown by the curve S_2—the inward shift will *not* offset the gain shown earlier; the net effect will be diminished, but not reversed. However, if the opportunity cost is large relative to the cost savings, the net effect can be reversed, as shown by the curve S_3.

7. *Impacts of government revenues*

The type of economic incentive programme used clearly has important implications for taxpayers. Auctioned allowances and taxes both can generate large sums for the government's treasury; the gains from the government's perspective are essentially the mirror image of the losses from the perspectives of the affected firms and their customers.

The ultimate distributional impacts of the changes in government revenue depend upon what the government does with the money. The basic alternatives are to increase spending or to reduce other revenues. Spending might be earmarked for specific purposes—including environmental purposes—or simply increased without specific programmes in mind (see OECD 1991a). A specific tax might be lowered, or all taxes lowered in response to the increased tax or allowance revenue. Note that since these other taxes tend to distort behaviour, while an effluent tax or allowance revenue correct distortions, there can be a net welfare gain from the switch in funding sources (see Terkla 1984).

B. Analyses of transitional costs

Transitional impacts are less prominent in economic policy evaluations although they often figure prominently in the public debate. This section provides an overview of the nature of transition costs and the analyses of their potential magnitudes.

1. Concept of transition costs

Transition costs represent the costs that accrue to households as a result of the process of adjustment from one regulatory regime to another (see Baumol and Oates 1988). During that period of adjustment, some resources become unemployed or lose substantial amounts of their value. As noted, in the long-run we assume that full (or approximately full) employment is reestablished and a net equilibrium set of wages and prices is established. Nevertheless, in the transition period the short-run costs to the unemployed could be substantial.

The size of these transition costs will depend in part on the market conditions. Decreases in output—and thus increases in transitional costs—will tend to be larger for firms involved in national or international markets. Since prices do not adjust, an increase in (real or opportunity) costs is reflected only in a decrease in output. The result is a decline in the demand for labour in that industry and a resulting increase in transition costs. In contrast, firms operating in local markets will have opportunities to pass at least some costs to customers in the form of higher prices, resulting in smaller reductions in output and fewer transitional costs.

Transitional costs thus tend to be larger the more the policy is focused on a particular geographic area. Imposing an effluent charge on a single waterway would tend to put firms there at a competitive disadvantage, with the result that production and employment would tend to decline (at least initially) in that region. Similarly, imposing an emissions tax in single country would tend to shift production and jobs in industries that operate largely in international markets to other countries, creating transitional costs for businesses and workers.

The size of the transition costs will depend as well on labour market conditions. Costs may be quite low if the transitionally unemployed are part of a large and vibrant labour market, where they can easily be absorbed. In contrast, the costs might be quite high if the workers are in isolated labour markets with few alternatives. The familiar story of the plight of workers in a "company town" when the company closes down illustrates how traumatic the adjustment can be. Such workers must often move to other areas to find work, moves that often are made only after considerable (and costly) search. The net result is a high level of transition costs in these circumstances.

2. Importance of benchmark

The size of transition costs will depend upon the benchmark used to compare economic instruments. Transition costs are large when economic instruments are compared to a "no regulation" benchmark. Some industries will invariably reduce operations in response to the increased costs imposed by economic instruments, even under the case of grandfathered allowances. The effects on different industries are likely to vary enormously. Given the focus of most economic incentive programmes on large stationary sources, the industries affected are likely to be chemical, electric utility, oil refining, and other "heavy" industries. That means that workers in those industries may face the transitional costs that come as the economy adjusts.

The direction of transition costs is less clear under the comparative approach. It is not clear whether economic instruments or command-and-control regulations lead to greater transition impacts. There are two offsetting effects:

- economic instruments decrease *control* costs and provide greater flexibility to businesses, thereby reducing the transitional impacts; but

- economic instruments create opportunity costs for *residual emissions* (either directly from allowance or tax payments or indirectly from the ability to sell allowances) that tend to increase the transitional impacts.

The net effect of these two offsetting effects on business costs (and thus transitional costs) is an empirical proposition.

The criterion often used by regulators to set command-and-control standards, however, suggests that economic instruments may in fact lead to more transitional costs. As noted in Chapter 2, emission standards are often set on the basis of "affordability," (i.e., the ability of the firm to pay for emission control equipment without closing down or substantially reducing production). This affordability criterion can be interpreted as the aim of preventing (or reducing) transition costs. Under this criterion, standards would be tighter for firms in local markets with the ability to pass costs on to their customers (i.e., "afford" the costs) and looser for firms in national or international markets with little ability to pass costs on. Moreover, marginal firms in any industry would tend to get more lenient standards. The net result would be few identifiable firms closing down (or substantially reducing production) because of command-and-control regulations. Although the overall economic costs may be very large, typically they will be less visible.

3. Incidence for transitional impacts

How will different income (or other) groups be affected by these transitional costs? As noted above, the transitional costs are likely to be highly localized geographically, falling with greatest force on those in smaller factor markets. Such costs would be incurred both by businesses (whose capital value is decreased) and by employees.

The income distributional pattern for workers will depend upon the changes in demand for low-income and high-income employees as a result of the transitions. In theory, the burdens might fall heavily on high-income workers, if the plants that are closed employ a relatively large proportion of executives and highly paid technical workers. However, as Baumol and Oates (1988) point out, it seems likely that costs will fall most heavily on those in the lower income groups. Higher-paid professional workers typically have greater occupational and geographic mobility than lower income workers. Indeed, the general concerns expressed about plant closings and the loss of "badly needed" jobs imply a general view that the more vulnerable members of society may lose the most from these transitional impacts.

C. Summary of steps in estimating distributive impacts

The most important conceptual task in designing a distributive analysis for economic instruments is likely to be clarifying the issues to be considered. As we have emphasized, the nature of the analysis depends critically on the benchmark and on whether or not government revenues are generated.

Most distributional analyses focus on households in different income groups. As noted, other groups might be of interest to some policy makers (e.g., racial groups, geographic subareas). Fortunately, the general methodology for estimating these distributional effects is applicable to all groupings. The general approach to estimating impacts by income groups is to use the income profile of purchasers of the goods and services whose prices are affected by regulations to measure burdens for consumers. These price effects are supplemented by estimates of the likely burdens of changes in corporate profits and also corporate profits taxes. Corporate profits are typically assumed to be affected at a national level even if the cost increases are local. (The following chapter illustrates how these various calculations have been performed in actual studies.)

The key steps in a distributive analysis can be summarized as follows:

1. Determine change in compliance costs (i.e., control costs plus any costs to pay taxes or purchase allowances) by industry.

2. Determine impacts of changes in compliance costs and "opportunity costs" on product prices and output, by industry.

3. Determine impacts of the price and output changes on "transitional costs" to workers in the relevant geographic groups (i.e., determine how many workers might become unemployed in the short-term due to output changes in the region).

4. Determine impacts of higher product prices on consumers in different income groups, based upon expenditure survey data.

5. Determine impacts of price and output changes on firm profits, by industry.

6. Determine the division of changes in firm profits between stockholders and taxpayers (in countries with corporate profits taxes).

7. Allocate the shareholder and taxpayer changes to income groups based upon survey data on their shares of corporate profits and income taxes, respectively.

8. If government revenues are collected, allocate them to income categories based upon the same survey data showing the share of income taxes paid by each income group. (Modify this step if the revenues are targeted to reduce specific taxes or to pay for new programmes).

9. Sum the results of the price impacts, the shareholder impacts and the taxpayer impacts for each income group.

10. Summarize the results of the analyses for income groups, workers, and regions.

The conceptual framework for assessing the incidence of long-term costs and benefits follows the series of steps that has been used for many years to estimate the impacts of tax and other public programmes. There are no conceptual hurdles. The distributive impacts of transitional impacts, less often studied, also present no major conceptual difficulties. However, as discussed in the following chapter, the data requirements for these analyses can be substantial.

Chapter 5

Empirical Evidence on the Distributive
Implications of Economic Instruments

The empirical information on the distributive impacts of environmental policies and economic instruments is quite sparse. However, in the last two years there have been a number of studies of carbon tax proposals that have included information on the distributive impacts of economic instruments. Like most other studies, these recent studies focus on income groups although information is sometimes provided for impacts on others, such as industry and geographic groups.

This chapter begins with a discussion of studies that have estimated the distributive impacts of command-and-control regulations. Emission tax studies are then considered, which, as noted, tend to be dominated by the recent carbon tax proposals. The final section considers the distributive studies of emissions trading programmes and proposals.

A. Distributional impacts of environmental policies

It is not surprising that there is little empirical information on the distributional impacts of most environmental programmes. As noted in the previous chapter, assessing both the cost and benefit distributions of environmental programmes can be complex. Most economic evaluations focus on the overall costs and benefits, avoiding these complexities. Nevertheless, there are a number of studies that provide indications of the likely patterns for control costs and environmental benefits.[20]

1. Cost burdens

a) Long-term costs

The empirical studies typically use the partial equilibrium framework—following the tax incidence model discussed in the previous chapter—to partition the long-term regulatory costs between consumers and producers. The burden by income group is the sum of consumer, stockholder and taxpayer burdens. For example, Harrison (1974) estimates the income distribution impacts of federal automotive emission controls in the United States by predicting changes in prices for new and used cars resulting from regulatory costs. Similar studies have been done for other environmental programmes (see e.g., Dorfman and Snow 1975; Freeman 1972; or Peskin 1978).

These studies generally find that pollution control costs are regressive, i.e., the percentage burden is greater for lower income households than for higher income households. For example, Peskin finds that the overall costs of an air pollution control programme ranged from 8.2 percent for the lowest income group to 1.8 percent for the highest income group. This pattern is also apparent in European studies (see e.g., Johnson et al. 1990; or Pearson and Smith 1991).

Similar results are obtained for control costs that fall initially on raw materials and intermediate goods. These costs affect households indirectly as a result of their eventual impacts on product and factor prices. Estimating these indirect effects requires a more complex model, usually built around an input-output table, to determine the influences of changes in raw material and intermediate goods on the prices of final products. For example, Robison (1985) uses a general-equilibrium framework, including a highly disaggregated input-output model, to determine the income distribution impacts of industrial pollution control costs. (His model assumes that all control costs are passed forward in the form of higher prices.) Average cost burdens were calculated for twenty income groups. He finds that the costs are highly regressive. Costs as a percentage of income range from 1.1 percent of income for the lowest income group to only 0.2 percent of income for the highest income group.

A smaller number of studies has estimated the distributional effects of environmental controls *among* plants and firms within an industry. Nichols and Harrison (1990b) show that there are large variations in costs among electric generation plants within a single utility. Leone and Jackson (1981) show that cost increases can differ substantially among plants subject to the same water pollution control requirements. (These issues are also discussed in Leone 1986.) Depending upon where these plants are in the overall distribution of costs within the industry, some plants may actually find that price increases exceed their cost increases. That is, those plants actually *gain* from regulations because those regulations impose *greater* costs on their competitors. Since the empirical evidence is quite limited, it is difficult to assess the importance of such intra-industry effects and their effect on price and output changes (and thus the final incidence of control costs).

b) Transition costs

Issues of job gains and losses figure prominently in the political debate over environmental policies. There are, however, relatively few published studies on the methodologies and results behind the estimates used in these debates. Some estimates appear to be partial estimates, based upon a subset of the overall effects of environmental controls. Harrison (1988) provides an overview of the potential regional employment impacts of air quality controls and estimates potential job losses for an extensive air quality plan developed for the Los Angeles air basin.

Although the focus is usually on the jobs that might be *lost* during a transition when regulations change, new regulatory requirements will of course add jobs as well. For example, a study of the United States acid rain programme estimates the additional jobs that would be created for pollution control equipment and related activities (Industrial Gas Cleaning Institute 1990). Whether such jobs compensate for transitional losses depends upon their respective timing and location.

2. Environmental benefits

The distributional impacts of environmental programmes will depend both upon the distribution of physical changes in environmental quality and upon the valuation that households place on those changes. Most studies focus on the physical effects.

The empirical studies find that environmental programmes targeted in urban areas result in greater per household physical benefits for lower income households. Air quality is typically worse in central areas where low income households tend to be over represented (see Baumol and Oates 1979). For example, Zupan (1973) found that poorer families tended to reside in areas of lower air quality in the New York region. Asch and Seneca (1979) found the same pattern, as did Freeman (1972) for three urban areas. In the United States, urban air pollution programmes tend to lead to either proportional reductions in all areas or greater reductions in more polluted areas. That means that the poor tend to get a disproportionate share of the physical benefits. For example, Harrison (1974) finds that the air quality benefits of the United States automotive controls are distributed in a pro-poor manner (i.e., greater physical benefits for lower income groups) in urban areas. Peskin (1978) also finds that benefits are distributed in a pro-poor manner.

There are, however, wide variations in the benefits for households in different geographic areas. The rural poor receive very few benefits from national programmes and pay substantial costs. For example, Harrison (1974) shows that rural households receive small benefits from federal automotive emission control, but pay large control costs because they have high levels of automotive ownership. Applied to rural areas where air quality is already quite good, federal air pollution controls therefore tend to be both inefficient (i.e., costs exceed benefits) and especially burdensome to the poor.[21]

Even for urban air quality benefits, however, there are two reasons to suspect that the final distribution of benefits could be substantially less pro-poor than the physical benefits suggest:

- Some of the benefits that initially accrue to renters will eventually accrue to owners, who tend to have considerably higher average incomes; and

- Lower income households may place a lower value on environmental benefits than higher income households.

For example, Harrison and Rubinfeld (1978b) find that lower income households place a lower value on air quality improvements, based upon a study of housing prices and air quality valuation in Boston. Similar results have been reported by Gianessi et al. (1979). These results are consistent with questionnaire results (see Baumol and Oates 1988).

What are the net distributive effects of existing regulations, taking into account both the costs and benefits? On balance, environmental regulations probably provide greater *net* benefits to higher income households than to lower income households (see Baumol and Oates 1988.) Costs tend to be regressive and benefits tend to be much less pro-poor than the physical changes suggest when differences in rents and valuation are taken into account.

B. Distributive impacts of emission tax schemes

Even less information is available on the distributional implications of economic incentive programmes, although as noted there have been a number of recent studies of carbon tax proposals. Table IV provides a summary of several studies that have estimated the distributional impacts of emission tax programmes. It is useful to distinguish the studies that investigate the impacts of a national tax from those that model the results of a global tax programme.

Table IV. Empirical studies of emissions taxes

Year	Reference	Pollutant	Country	Groups	Results[a]
National Taxes					
1990	United States CBO	carbon	United States	Industry	Varied
1991	DeWitt et al.	carbon	United States	Region	Varied
1991	Osten et al.	energy	Canada	Region	Varied
1991	Pearson and Smith	carbon	Six European	Income	Varied
1991	Poterba	CO_2	United States	Income	Regressive
1991	Scott	carbon	Ireland	Income	Regressive
1992	Shah and Larsen	carbon	Pakistan	Income	Varied
International Taxes					
1990	Howarth et al.	carbon	World	Region	Varied
1990	Whalley and Wigle	carbon	World	Region	Varied
1991	Hoeller et al.	carbon	World	Region	Varied

Note: [a] Results are impacts relative to "no regulation."

1. National emission taxes

a) Income distributional impacts

Poterba (1991) analyzes the income distributional impacts of a $100 carbon tax on households in the United States using the general methodology outlined in the previous chapter. His analysis assumes full forward pass through of the tax to energy prices, resulting in increases in retail prices of gasoline and fuel oil prices of 25 percent and 27 percent, respectively. Natural gas prices were projected to rise by 23 percent, while the retail price of coal rises by 114 percent. Retail electricity prices were projected to rise by 36 percent. These price changes were combined with data on household energy expenditures to estimate the distributional burdens of the carbon tax.

Figure 11 presents Poterba's results showing cost burdens as a share of both income and expenditures for households broken into ten income or expenditure groups. (Poterba suggests that a household's expenditures are a better measure of its lifetime income than is its annual income.) The pattern is regressive using both measures, although the degree of regressivity is much smaller when expenditures are used. The difference in measured impact is particularly dramatic for the lowest income group. The lowest group is projected to pay more than 10 percent of income due to the tax, but only 3.7 percent of outlays. If expenditures are a better measure of lifetime income, the expenditure results would provide a more accurate indication of the long-run regressivity of a carbon tax. These results indicate that households in the three lowest expenditure groups would face burdens averaging 3.7 percent of income; in contrast, households in the three highest expenditure groups would average only 2.6 percent of outlays.

Figure 12. **Income distribution impacts of a carbon tax in the United States**

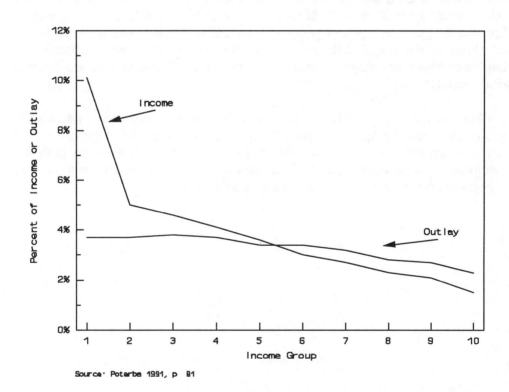

Source: Poterba 1991, p 81

The results in Figure 11 do not provide complete estimates of the income distributional impacts of a carbon tax. Poterba points out the following limitations of his estimates:

- *General equilibrium effects.* The results ignore the effects of higher fossil fuel prices on the prices of energy-intensive products, such as steel and automobiles. While smaller than the direct effects, these second-order effects will influence the distributional pattern.

- *Asset market effects.* Returns to intermediaries (such as oil refineries) would fall, which would reduce profits for oil companies and others. Given the income profile of stockholders, this effect would reduce the regressivity of the carbon tax.

- *Macroeconomic effects and transition costs.* If the carbon tax results in unemployment, as most models predict, lower income groups might face greater transition costs if they were more likely to become unemployed.

Poterba also points out that policy makers would be likely to take actions to reduce the regressivity of a carbon tax.

Schillo et al. (1992) report the results of estimating the distributional impacts of a carbon tax in the United States using a general equilibrium modelling framework. The paper presents the draft results of using three macroeconomic modelling approaches to measure the impacts of imposing a carbon tax and directing the tax revenues to alternative uses. The alternative uses include debt reduction or reduction in other forms of taxation. The results indicate that a carbon tax that starts at $15 per ton and grows by 5 percent per year in real dollars would have a small, slightly regressive impact. However, the analysis indicates that this slight regressivity can be offset by various tax recycling mechanisms or changes in transfer programmes. (These options are discussed in the following chapter).

Pearson and Smith (1991) provide information on the distributional impacts of a carbon tax imposed in various European countries.[22] Approximately one-half of energy is used directly by households and the other half by industry and related sectors. The authors present empirical information on the distributive impacts of the taxes that would fall on household directly through greater payments for domestic energy and automotive fuels.[23]

Figure 13. **Income distribution impacts of a carbon tax in the United Kingdom**

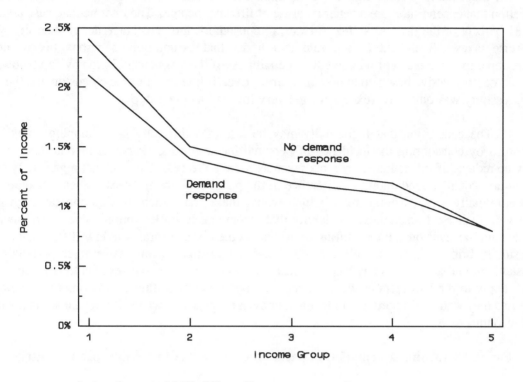

Source: Pearson and Smith 1991, p. 42.

? shows the distributional pattern by income quintile in the United Kingdom for the direct household costs for a carbon tax equivalent to $10 per barrel. Two lines are shown, one excluding any response to higher prices and the other showing the results when a simulation model is used to reflect behavioral responses to higher energy prices. The two sets of figures are very similar and show the same pattern: a carbon tax would be regressive. When responses to the increased prices are taken into account, the percentage burden ranges from 2.1 percent of income for households in the lowest quintile to 0.8 percent for those in the highest quintile, a difference of a factor of three. Ignoring price responses, the range is somewhat larger, from 2.4 percent to 0.8 percent.[24]

Figure 13, also taken from Pearson and Smith (1991) shows that the distributive pattern is very different for other European countries. In five of the six countries, the percentage burden of carbon tax payments for household energy use is only weakly related to income, if at all. Ireland is the only country with a regressive pattern similar to the United States and United Kingdom (Scott 1991 finds a similar pattern in Ireland.) Pearson and Smith note that the less regressive pattern in these other countries reflects both differences in energy spending as well as differences in the consumption of fuels with high carbon content.

The study by Shah and Larsen (1992) of the World Bank suggests that the regressivity of a carbon tax may be even less of a concern in developing countries. The authors prepare estimates of the impacts of a carbon tax on households in Pakistan. Three sets of estimates are prepared based upon different assumptions regarding the percentage of the tax shifted forward to consumers. For each set, the authors present figures based upon income and expenditures, following Poterba's indication that expenditures are a better measure of lifetime income. The intermediate case assumed that 31 percent of the tax was shifted forward to consumers, the percentage determined in a study of excise taxes. Shah and Larsen find that under that assumption, a carbon tax would be proportional to income and progressive to expenditures. If the tax were all borne by capital owners, it would be progressive based upon both measures. Even if it were all borne by customers, the level of regressivity was quite low (except for the very lowest income group).

The conclusion that regressivity may be less of a difficulty in developing countries is reinforced by considering the incidence of personal income taxes. Personal income taxes would likely be reduced if substantial carbon tax revenues were collected. Thus, the net regressivity of the carbon tax would depend upon the difference in the patterns between the two taxes. Income taxes are traditionally seen as progressive, which would make the switch to a carbon tax regressive. However, Shah and Larsen present evidence that income taxes are less progressive when one takes into account tax evasion and the shifting of urban income taxes to rural workers. Tax evasion tends to result in bribes paid by middle class businessmen to high income government officials. In Pakistan, only urban workers pay income taxes. However, the income taxes lead to reduced wages, which apply to rural workers as well. In sum, the net effect of adding a carbon tax in developing countries may well be proportional to income, or even progressive, when all relevant shifts are taken into account.

Figure 14. **Income distribution impacts of a carbon tax in six European countries**

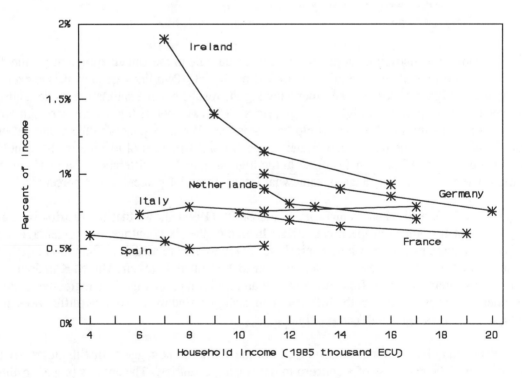

Source: Pearson and Smith 1991, p. 43.

92

b. Geographic and industrial impacts

A carbon tax in the United States would have dramatically different impacts in different regions. The high carbon content of coal means that coal consuming and producing regions would face much greater costs and transitional dislocations. According to a recent Congressional Budget Office study, a phased-in carbon tax of $100 per ton would result in a 13 percent reduction in coal use by the year 2000 (see Stavins and Whitehead 1992). Using the results of a partial equilibrium model of the tax burden based upon household purchases of energy, DeWitt et al. (1991) find that the burden of a carbon tax can vary by a factor of as much as 50 percent among the nine United States Census regions. These results reflect regional differences in electric generation technologies, energy prices, and household characteristics.

Osten et al. (1991) present the results of a macroeconomic evaluation of alternative energy taxes in Canada. Their results include evaluations of the differential impacts on different provinces. Not surprisingly, Alberta (the major coal-producing province) faces the largest declines in output (and other measures) under a carbon tax.

2. International carbon tax

Hoeller et al. (1991) and OECD (1992a) summarize the results of empirical studies that have modeled the impacts of carbon taxes on national and regional world economies. The results do not deal with income distributional impacts, but the regional results make it clear that carbon taxes orchestrated at an international level can have vastly different impacts on different regions of the world depending upon how they are structured. (See Barrett 1991 and Barrett 1992 for analyses of the various issues associated with structuring an international global warming tax, including the possibility of side payments to countries harmed by the tax.)

Howarth et al. (1990) model the effects of an international carbon tax, estimating the differential impacts on different country groups. They conclude that the burden of a global tax would fall much more heavily (in percentage terms) on developing regions. To avoid these effects, the authors suggest delaying restrictions on those countries until the relevant technology could be transferred from developed countries and the impacts could be reduced.

Table V summarizes the results of the study by Whalley and Wigle (1990) of the welfare losses to various world regions under the following alternatives:

- a production-based carbon tax collected by national governments;

- a consumption-based carbon tax collected by national governments;

- a global carbon tax collected by an international body with the receipts redistributed according to population; and

- national consumption taxes that resulted in the same per capita consumption of fossil fuels.

All four policies are designed to achieve a 50 percent reduction in global carbon emissions. Note that the overall costs of the options range from an average welfare loss of 2.1 percent in the case of the national consumption taxes to a loss of 8.5 percent when the per capita ceiling on fossil fuels is imposed. These differences reflect the large divergence from efficiency when a per capita ceiling is imposed.

But the distributive results are even more dramatic. Naturally, the greatest swings occur for oil exporters; their impacts range from a gain of 4.5 percent under the production tax to a loss of 16.7 percent under the system of national consumption taxes. But the swings for North America are also large; North American residents would face welfare impacts of 1.2 percent for the most efficient policy but would see a loss of 18.6 percent in welfare under the per capita ceiling.

Table V. **Regional welfare changes under alternative carbon tax policies**

	National Production Taxes	National Consumption Taxes	Global Production Tax[a]	Per Capita Emission Ceiling
EC	-4.0	1.4	-3.8	-6.4
North America	-4.3	-1.2	-9.8	-18.6
Japan	-3.7	3.0	-0.9	-2.5
Oil exporters	4.5	-16.7	-13.0	-15.1
Developing countries	-7.1	-4.5	1.8	-1.2
World	-4.4	-2.1	-4.2	-8.5

Notes: Hicksian equivalent variation over the period 1990-2030 in 1990 prices as a per cent of GDP in present value terms.
        [a] Redistribution proportional to each region's population.
Source: Whalley and Wigle (1990) as cited in Hoeller et al. (1991).

The range of impacts for developing countries is smaller, but the changes might imply even greater equity impacts. Under a system of national production taxes, developing countries would face a 7.1 percent loss in welfare. In contrast, if a global production tax were combined with population-based redistribution, the welfare of developing countries would increase by 1.8 percent.

Hoeller et al. (1991) point out that the parameter values on which the developing country impacts are based (in all studies, not just that of Whalley and Wigle) are highly uncertain. The extremely inefficient use of energy resources, particularly in the centrally-planned economies, means that there may be very large scope for reducing fossil fuel use at lower costs than implied by these models. Nevertheless, an international tax on carbon would inevitably hit the poorer countries hard unless it were combined with some redistribution of revenues.

C. Distributional impacts of emissions trading schemes

A number of distributive analyses have been done of marketable permits programmes or proposals in the United States. Table VI summarizes the results of some of these studies. These include studies of programmes for air pollution, water pollution, and noise.

Table VI. Empirical studies of emission trading

Year	Reference	Pollutant	Geographic	Groups
1977	David et al.	Water, Phos.	Wisconsin	Income
1980	Palmer et al.	Air/CFC	USA	Industry
1982	Hahn & Noll	Air/SO_X	Los Angeles	Geography Income
1983	Harrison	Aircraft Noise	USA (Boston Logan Airport	Geography Income
1989	ICF	SO_2	USA	Labor Geography
1992	Harrison & Nichols	ROG/NO_X	Los Angeles Basin	Labor Industry

The distributional studies of emissions trading schemes tend to focus on differences in the impacts across regions and industries, rather than across income groups. This different focus probably reflects the differences in benchmarks used to evaluate emission tax and emission trading programmes:

- emission tax evaluations typically use a "no regulation" baseline and assume that large government revenues will be collected; the result is *increase* in overall business costs for emissions taxes; and

- emission trading evaluations use a command-and-control benchmark and assume that allowances will be grandfathered and thus that no government revenues will be collected; the net result is *reductions* in overall costs for emissions trading programmes.

These different benchmarks mean that, in contrast to emission taxes, the impacts of emissions trading are generally viewed as favourable to the poor, since control costs are reduced. Indeed, given the regressive pattern of control costs, lower income households are likely to gain the most. (As noted in Chapter 4, this pro-poor result may not hold if the opportunity cost of allowances results in price increases.) Most distributive studies therefore focus on potentially vulnerable regions and industries.

1. *Geographic impacts*

The analysis of the United States acid rain programme performed during the debate over the 1990 Clean Air Act provides an example of a geographic and industry analysis of emissions trading programmes. ICF (1989) provides information on the impacts of the (then proposed) trading programme on electricity rates by state and coal production by region. The study finds that the pattern of regional coal production would change substantially under trading. Future coal mining employment declines significantly in high-sulphur coal regions and increases in low-sulphur coal regions, as a result of the shift to Western low-sulphur coal mines that generally have higher productivities. Figure 14 shows the estimated pattern shifts in 1995 (when the first phase of reductions would begin) and in 2000 (when the second and final phase of reductions would apply).

Figure 15. **Impacts of acid rain trading program on coal mining employment**

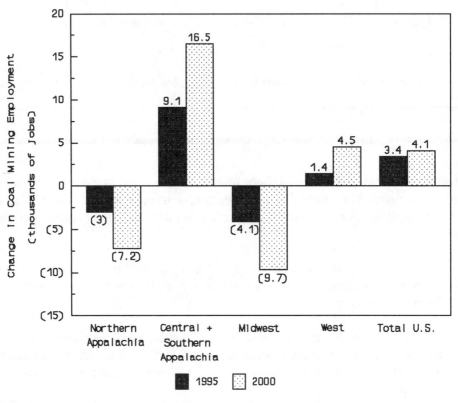

Source· ICF 1989, Table A-10

2. Industry impacts

a) Overall impacts

Most of the studies listed in Table VI find that overall business costs increase (relative to traditional regulations) under an emissions trading programme with auctioned allowances. Put another way, the savings in compliance costs from trading are overwhelmed by government payments for the initial allowances. The cost increases can be substantial. The Palmer et al. (1980) study of chlorofluorocarbon trading estimates that the present value of transfer payments from firms to the government would be between $1.2 and $1.7 billion (1976 dollars). Harrison (1983) estimates that a national aircraft noise charge with a baseline (no-charge level) of 98 decibels would generate about $150 million per year in revenue. The wealth transfers from other programmes are even more dramatic because they are focused locally. For example, Hahn and Noll estimate that a trading scheme for SO_2 in the Los Angeles basin would yield $150 million per year in transfers.

These studies also shed light on the situation in which savings in compliance costs would exceed transfer payments or "opportunity costs." The net effect depends primarily upon the stringency of control. The water pollution and CFC cases illustrate the two extreme cases. Government payments are small in the water pollution case because municipalities are required to remove 85 percent of the pollution, and thus only 15 percent was previously "owned" by cities that must now buy allowances. In contrast, the CFC plan evaluated by Palmer et al. only reduced CFCs by 15 percent, and thus government payments dominated compliance costs; overall the transfer payments were about 14 times the costs of actually reducing emissions.

b) Differences among firms

Some distributive studies also evaluate the difference in compliance costs among firms. Table VII shows the differences in compliance costs for industries affected by the CFC emissions trading plan. Although overall compliance costs fall by 77.5 percent overall under the hypothetical trading scheme, these costs increase by 22 percent for solvent manufacturers. In contrast, compliance costs fall for flexible foam and rigid foam manufacturers by 64 percent and 35 percent, respectively. Although these estimates do not take into account likely price changes, they do illustrate the large variations among firms in the effects of the trading programme.

Trading programmes are often supported by large firms, which stand to gain substantially simply because of the scale of their operations and emissions. Smaller firms or industries are often suspicious, both because they tend to be less familiar with economic instruments and because they worry that the larger firms will tend to use emissions trading to drive them out of business. The trading plan developed by the United States EPA in the mid-1980's to deal with the phase-down in lead in gasoline faced this obstacle when it was announced (Harrison and Nichols 1990b). A study of experience showed, however, that both large and small refineries gained and anti-competitive abuses did not surface (Hahn and Hester 1989).

The trading programme being developed in the Los Angeles, California air basin is facing similar objections from small businesses. That programme is designed to create markets for three key pollutants in the Los Angeles Basin. (The Appendix provides a summary of this programme.) An empirical study showed that the trading programme would reduce overall control costs by at least

Table VII. **Changes in compliance costs for industries under a CFC marketable permit scheme**

Product Area	Cumulative Effects of Economic Incentives		Deviation from Mandatory Controls	
	Emissions Reduction (millions of permit pounds)	Compliance Cost ($1976 millions)	Emissions Reduction (millions of permit pounds)	Compliance Cost (percent)
Flexible Foam	380.7	$29.2	-120.5	-64.1%
Solvents	390.3	67.3	+204.6	+21.6
Rigid Foam	26.7	3.8	-79.4	-35.0
Retail Food	18.3	7.3	--	--
Chillers	1.0	0.1	--	--
Total	816.9	$107.8	+4.6	-77.5%

Source: Palmer et al. (1980, p. 223), as cited in Harrison and Portney (1982).

40 percent relative to the "command-and-control" programme (Harrison and Nichols 1992a). However, small businesses were concerned that they would not share in the cost savings and would be harmed by switching to an emissions trading regime. Harrison and Nichols (1992a) investigated the impacts on small businesses, using a case study of a single industry, furniture manufacturing.

Figure 15 shows the key results from that case study. (These results are discussed in detail in the Appendix.) Under the traditional regulatory approach—shown as "AQMP cost" in Figure 15 —furniture manufacturers are estimated to pay about $18 million per year in control costs. However, if they were allocated the same emissions as the implicitly receive with traditional controls and are given the possibility of selling additional controlled tons, furniture manufacturers as a group would actually gain more than $31 million per year (the RECLAIM case in Figure 15). The reason is simple: the industry is composed of firms with relatively low control costs; the firms reap large profits from selling emissions reductions.

Figure 16. **The Los Angeles Trading Programme provides a net gain to the furniture industry when the initial allocation is the same as traditional controls**

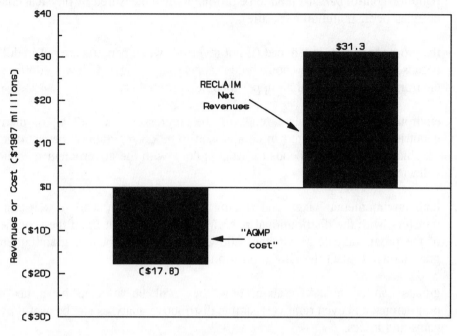

Source: Harrison and Nichols 1992, p. 59.

This study thus illustrates the potential mistakes groups can make if they do not do a careful empirical study. However, the study also showed that the impacts on different industries will differ dramatically depending upon how the initial allowances are allocated. This latter point is evident in other studies as well (see Harrison and Portney 1982).

D. Summary of empirical studies

Relatively few empirical analyses have been done on the distributive impacts of environmental programmes, and even fewer have been done for economic instruments. The reasons for this paucity of empirical studies are not hard to fathom. Assessing the distributive patterns is complicated. Moreover, the lack of a widely accepted framework for structuring the analysis means that the various studies cannot necessarily be compared.

Nevertheless, the available studies do appear to show common patterns. The following are the major conclusions:

- pollution control *costs* tend to be regressive, i.e., the percentage burden is greater for lower income households than for higher income households;

99

- the regressivity is reduced when income is measured by expenditures (a proxy for long-term income) rather than by current income;

- pollution control *benefits* tend to be pro-poor when measured by physical changes (e.g., changes in air pollution exposure);

- the pro-poor pattern is reduced (if not reversed) when benefits are put in dollar values, because lower income households appear to place a lower dollar value on environmental benefits than upper income households;

- environmental taxes also tend to be regressive—at least in many OECD countries—when measured in comparison to a "no regulation" benchmark, although the final pattern also depends on what is done with the government revenues that are collected;

- both environmental taxes and trading programmes can lead to substantial wealth transfers, with the distributional pattern highly dependent upon the specific elements of the programme (e.g., whether allowances are auctioned or grandfathered and, if grandfathered, what the allocation formula is);

- groups can be mistaken about how they will be affected by a tax or trading programme; and even relatively simple distributive analyses can be useful in clarifying gains and losses.

Perhaps the overarching conclusion from these empirical studies is that an empirical distributional analysis is important to clarify what is at stake when economic instruments are adopted. Given the novelty of the approach, it is easy to be mistaken about the impacts of emissions taxes and emissions trading programmes.

Chapter 6

Mitigating Distributive Impacts

Virtually all desirable policies create losers as well as winners. The clearest cases are those put out of work during the transition to the new policy. But others might lose as well. Although cost savings can lower prices and increase output in the longer run, some prices may increase due to tax or "opportunity cost" effects. What is done with any revenues will also affect the pattern of gains and losses.

In short, there will be groups that lose under economic incentive schemes. These groups are likely to argue that they should be compensated for losses suffered. This chapter discusses the issues surrounding policies to compensate those affected by policy changes.

A. Should compensation be paid?

There are two major reasons to compensate those who might be affected by the use of economic incentives (see Harrison and Portney 1982 and Burtraw and Portney 1991). The first is pragmatic: potential losers might block a shift to economic incentives if they are not compensated. Losers are particularly likely to block a shift if they are relatively few in number and well organized, and those who gain are widely distributed and less well-organized.

A second reason is related to normative notions of equity: compensation is justified if losses fall on the less fortunate members of society. For example, if lower income groups sustain large job losses or incur large price increases, according to this criteria there would be a justification for developing means of compensating them. In sum, as Baumol and Oates (1988) point out, ignoring the distributive impacts of environmental policy may either unintentionally harm certain groups in society or undermine the political support for the policy.

Both of these rationales can be questioned. For example, some argue that account should not be taken of changes due to individual actions (such as economic instruments), but rather that overall equity policies should be formulated. Piecemeal compensation, according to this argument, would not be desirable. We should leave redistributional policy to be formulated separately, presumably taking into account all relevant considerations and not just those related to environmental policy or a specific case.[25]

Moreover, others have questioned the legitimacy of compensating those affected by increases in the stringency of environmental regulation. Consider the case of coal companies or their employees; does society have a special obligation to these individuals if new emission controls cause them to lose profits or jobs? Does the answer to this question depend upon whether the new controls were unexpected or a natural risk of doing business? Or should the government be guided by a "do not direct harm" rule that holds government to a higher standard regardless of whether the change was expected or not? (See Schultze 1977 and Burtraw and Portney 1991.)

Despite these objections, on balance it seems useful to consider methods of compensating those who lose from environmental regulation, or at least to acknowledge that groups that lose will press for compensation. There seems little reason to believe that some overarching redistributional policy will take into account the distributive effects of economic incentive schemes; and it would seem bad politics to assume that groups adversely affected will not make their concerns known.

The remainder of this chapter discusses what can and should be done to deal with distributive impacts, beginning with an overview of existing experience.

B. Experience with compensation

1. Mitigation versus Compensation

It is useful to distinguish between mitigation and compensation. Mitigation refers to reducing the impacts of the programme *ex ante* so that the potential impacts do not occur. For example, the government might reduce or eliminate a pollution control requirement because it would harm particular groups. Compensation refers to aid to particular groups *ex post* so that they are (at least partly) "made whole." For example,the government may go ahead with a policy it knows will harm workers in the region, but it will provide income support and training programmes to compensate.

2. Examples of existing mitigation policies

In the United States, mitigation is a common element of traditional environmental policy. As noted above, environmental statutes and regulations often base control requirements on "affordability"—the ability of the firms within an industry to pay for control equipment without going out of business or substantially reducing production. Thus, there is a built-in concern in environmental policy for the distributional effects on firms.

Moreover, as many authors have noted, the political process often leads to requirements that are implicitly based upon efforts to obtain advantages for particular groups (see e.g., Crandall 1983). For example, requirements to prevent "significant deterioration" in air quality in pristine areas were supported most vigorously by representatives of urban areas and Northeastern states. This pattern suggests that the built-up areas were using the requirement to make sure that firms in competitor regions faced similar control requirements. Ackerman and Hassler (1981) describe the setting of pollution standards for coal-fired power plants in the 1977 Clean Air Act Amendments as based largely upon a political need to protect the jobs of midwestern miners of high-sulfur coal.

Many more examples of mitigation strategies could be presented, but more examples do not seem necessary. The history of policy development is largely a history of mitigation strategies: designing policies that achieve their objectives while at the same time dealing with adverse impacts. Thus, rather than being an exception, designing policies with mitigation in mind is probably the norm.

3. Examples of existing compensation policies

All OECD countries have policies to compensate for hardships. Income support programmes are the most obvious examples. Those put out of work for whatever reason have access to some government assistance. Evaluating the extent and design of these compensation policies is not necessary for our purposes. It is useful to note (as Poterba 1991 points out) that many transfer programmes are already indexed for price changes. Since the final burden of many regulatory programmes is reflected in higher prices, indexed components of income will partly adjust to compensate for the additional tax burdens. Poterba reports that two thirds of the income received by households in the lowest expenditure decile is indexed; this high percentage reflects the importance of elderly families who receive social security as well as other transfer recipients in this group.

A full review of other, more focused compensation policies would be a major task. But it is clear that those who lose from government policy are sometimes compensated (Harrison and Portney 1982). Most examples seem based upon political necessity—the policy would not have been adopted without the compensation. For example, when Congress planned to expand California's Redwood National Park, the loggers who would lose their jobs as a result of decreased timber production constituted a vocal and easily identifiable group who would *lose* under tightening controls. To gain their support, Congress included a provision that offered the loggers an average of $6,000 per week during the early part of the programme (Goldfarb 1980).

Non-environmental examples of compensation include the Trade Adjustment Assistance Act, which provides supplements to regular unemployment compensation when joblessness results from lower trade barriers. Indeed, this programme has been extended to workers hurt by import competition even if no trade barriers had existed. Other examples include tax breaks to those affected by deregulation of trucking, and job training help for those affected by deregulation of the airlines.

Compensation has also been a common element of environmental policy. When the pathbreaking Clean Air Act and Clean Water Act were passed in the early 1970's, Congress created several compensation programmes to ease the transition to the more stringent requirements. The most direct programme was the federal subsidy programme for constructing municipal sewage treatment plants. In the 1970's, the EPA spent more than $20 billion in such subsidies. Congress has also helped firms. For example, federal laws permit firms to finance some pollution control using tax-exempt bonds, allowing them to obtain lower interest rates. Consumers are indirectly compensated by programmes that reduce the cost to firms of meeting environmental requirements. Fewer costs mean that price increases are smaller.

Direct compensation to workers affected by environmental regulation is not common. However, the EPA has an early warning system that is supposed to alert it to potential plant closings. The agency also has a programme to provide information to workers, firms and communities about federal assistance programmes. Moreover, because of the mitigation measures EPA uses to set rules—most notably the affordability standard—the agency claims that very few workers actually lose their jobs because of environmentally-related closures.

C. Mitigation options for economic instruments

There are a number of ways in which loses might be mitigated when economic instruments are used. A common tension is to avoid harm while at the same time maintaining the desirable features of the programme.

1. Emissions taxes

a) Cutoff

An apparently simple means of reducing the distributive impacts of emissions taxes would be to reduce revenues by setting a cutoff before the tax is levied. Reducing tax revenues by setting a threshold is, however, more complicated than one might think (Harrison 1989). Thresholds would have to be set for individual sources rather than total emissions, leading to the same complexities as setting individual emission standards. If the cutoffs were set on the same basis as standards (i.e., emissions per unit of output or input), the tax approach would lose some of its efficiency advantages. This is because firms would not have the most efficient incentives to reduce outputs or inputs (Nichols 1984). Moreover, as a practical matter, it would be extremely difficult to set thresholds that eliminated all tax payments, and thus at least some distributional impacts would occur.

b) Exemptions

A more common means of mitigating tax impacts is to create a system of exemptions similar to the exemptions for the food and clothing part of excise tax programmes in some jurisdictions. For example,the carbon tax recently proposed by the European Commission includes the possibility of a number of sectoral exemptions for highly energy-intensive industries, such as steel and cement (Pearson and Smith 1991). These exemptions were based upon the effects the tax would have on the international competitiveness of these sectors, and it has been suggested that the exemptions would be eliminated if other competitors (e.g., United States and Japan) adopted an equivalent carbon tax. Indeed, these adverse industrial effects are a major rationale for developing a comprehensive global policy on carbon.

The recently-enacted Swedish carbon tax programme provides a good example of the use of exemptions to mitigate potential competitiveness impacts (see Bohm 1991 and Brannlund and Kriström 1991). Swedish officials were concerned (with justification) that a substantial tax on carbon used to produce products sold in European (or world) markets would simply result in decreases in Swedish production and corresponding increases in production elsewhere. The result would be reduced employment in Sweden and little effect on the overall level of carbon emitted. One way of dealing with this problem would be to tax the carbon embedded in imports. But this can be difficult administratively. Sweden decided to put a cap on tax payments that has the effect of exempting key sectors from the carbon tax.

There are, however, reasons to question the desirability of such a mitigation strategy. Pearson and Smith (1991) point out three undesirable features of exemptions. First, exempting pollution-intensive industries would require a higher tax on other sectors in order to achieve a given target reduction in emissions. Second, the exemption distorts the structure of the economy toward pollution-intensive activities, the opposite of the objective of the tax in the first place. Third, the exemptions seem likely to become permanent measures of protection. Pearson and Smith note that it is not clear what policy measures would satisfy conditions for abolishing the exemptions. Creating such permanent protective measures (in the name of mitigation) might compromise both the objectives of a cost-effective pollution reduction policy and those of free trade.

2. Emissions trading

a) Allocation formula

It may be easier to develop mitigation measures in the case of emissions trading programmes—at least to deal with potential impacts on businesses—because valuable property rights can be given out. Emissions trading schemes have "natural" mechanisms for reducing or eliminating some of the distributional impacts that arise (Harrison and Portney 1982). As discussed earlier, if allowances are allocated free of change, rather than auctioned, the government can avoid the overall loss to businesses. Property rights are split, with firms "owning" the right to pollute up to the number of allowances issued.

A similar result can be achieved with a "zero-revenue auction" in which each firm receives an initial allocation, but is required to offer its entire allocation for sale in the auction (see Hahn and Noll 1982). This auction does not lead to government revenue, because the gross payments firms make are counterbalanced by the gross payments the government makes to the firms based upon the initial allocation.

Any formula for distributing allowances will of course lead to gainers and losers among individual polluting firms. Allowances are valuable commodities, as examples given in earlier chapters illustrated. Firms thus will have strong incentives to support allocation formulas that provide them with the maximum number of allowances. What is less obvious is that the allocation formula also will affect product prices, and thus the distribution of costs between firms and consumers as well as the possibility of transition costs to workers unemployed as a result of the market adjustments (see Nichols and Harrison 1991).

b) Conflicts with cost saving

As discussed above, allocation formulas based upon prior activity (e.g. historical emissions or output) have the effect of creating a fixed number of emissions allowances and also an "opportunity cost" when they are used. That opportunity cost is reflected in market conditions, either higher prices and/or reduced output. In contrast, if the allocation formula is based upon current or future actions, such as future output or emissions, no opportunity cost is created and firms do not gain the rents. That means that prices do not rise or output decline.

There is, therefore, a conflict between the efficiency of the emissions trading programme and avoidance of transitional costs (or larger consumer price impacts). A formula based upon future activities avoids the transitional and price impacts, but at the expense of a less efficient programme: the price of products would not reflect the value of reducing emissions. Conversely, an efficient policy in which allowances are initially allocated on an historical basis leads to rents to firms as well as output and price effects that might harm particular groups.

A more important obstacle to an effective and efficient emissions trading programme involves efforts to avoid closures by preventing firms from using "shut down credits." As discussed in the case study of the Los Angeles trading programme presented in the Appendix, labour groups proposed that firms not be allowed to use credits obtained from shutting down production facilities. However, such a policy would be virtually impossible to administer, since it would be virtually impossible to determine which firms shut down because of the trading programme, and would likely result in firms evading the prohibition by keeping skeleton staffs. Implementing such a policy to mitigate adverse effects therefore would likely be ineffective. If it did succeed in preventing layoffs, the strategy would be an inefficient means of dealing with the transition costs; any equity gains would be costly.

D. Compensation strategies

Compensation policies can create similar tensions between efficiency and equity. It is possible to compensate at least some of the individuals harmed by the use of economic incentives. But compensatory policies can compromise the objectives of economic incentive policies and can also create additional efficiency and equity concerns.

1. Emissions taxes

Although most emissions taxes are likely to be evaluated from an independent perspective, this does not mean that the distributive impacts will be ignored. Indeed, as Poterba (1991) points out, the recent history of tax policy in most industrial countries suggests that there is large political resistance to imposing higher taxes on the poor. In fact, virtually all discussions of carbon taxes consider means of compensating or neutralizing their distributional impacts.

a) Revenue neutrality

The most common compensatory approach is to make the taxes "revenue neutral," i.e., to offset increased emissions taxes with corresponding reductions in other taxes. For example, the European Commission proposals stress that the carbon tax should be revenue neutral. (The revenues would accrue to individual countries, which could of course decide whether to decrease taxes or increase public spending.) Similarly, the Swedish carbon tax was introduced as one element of tax reform, which left overall revenues unchanged.

As noted above, the tax codes of many countries have automatic elements of their income transfer programmes that compensate for some of the impacts through price level indexing. These programmes do not completely compensate, both because not all low income households affected are transfer recipients and because the expenditure patterns of low income households tend to put greater weight on energy outlays (Poterba 1991).

Reducing other taxes to gain revenue neutrality creates another tension between efficiency and equity objectives. As Pearce (1991) and others have pointed out, greater reliance on environmental taxes generally creates a more efficient tax structure; other taxes create distortions while environmental taxes reduce distortions. (Pearce refers to this as a "double dividend.") Terkla (1984) provides empirical estimates of the efficiency gains from substituting environmental taxes for the average set of United States taxes. Pearson and Smith (1991) report on a recent study suggesting that the marginal welfare effect of the United States tax structure is on the order of $0.20 to $.50 for every dollar raised. However, the most distortionary taxes are not those that burden the poor the most. Offsetting increased carbon taxes with reduced income taxes would reduce economic distortions but do little (if anything) to reduce the net regressivity.

b) Other compensation mechanisms

There are a host of options for using the tax system to compensate for regressive impacts (see, e.g., Poterba 1991, Pearson and Smith 1991, and Schillo 1992). For example, in the United States the earned income tax credit or the personal allowance could be increased, reducing the burden on low income households (but not reducing distortions in the tax system). The tax code could also be used to compensate for industrial burdens, either by reducing corporate income taxes or providing tax benefits for operating in areas hard hit by the carbon tax.

All of these tax changes suffer from a problem of targeting. That is, the offsetting gains tend not to accrue to precisely the individuals and households hurt by emissions taxes. Benefits to wage earners do not help those not working. Gains to businesses locating in an area help those relatively unaffected as well as those hard hit by a tax.

Several proposals have been made to improve the targeting of compensation. Some of these are tax-related. For example, Poterba (1991) suggests an explicit policy of tax credits for energy expenditures. Allowing each household a tax credit equal to some percentage of income devoted to purchasing energy would alter the average price of energy (and reduce the regressivity) while still preserving the efficiency value of a higher marginal price. Providing energy programmes to the elderly may be justified because of their greater home heating expenditures.

Other policies might target those put out of work. These could include stimulating new businesses in affected areas, relocating labour to areas with more robust labour markets, training programmes to give workers new skills, increasing government spending in the regions, or even takeover of failed operations. Although some of these measures are likely to be cost-effective, experience suggests that such policies often generate relatively few gains.

None of these policies will perfectly target those affected by emissions taxes. And, indeed, there are reasons for not wanting perfect targeting. Why should a worker put out of work because of a carbon tax be treated substantially different than a worker put out of work because of other business conditions? Given the difficulty of determining what factors "cause" such dislocations, it may not even be feasible to make such comparisons. It may well be better—more efficient and more equitable—to provide general compensatory programmes rather than ones only available to those harmed by tax-related impacts.

2. *Emissions trading programmes*

The ability to mitigate business losses through grandfathering of allowances and choosing an appropriate allocation formula means that compensation issues relating to business or consumer losses are less relevant for emissions trading programmes. Under the comparative perspective that dominates most evaluations, trading programmes save costs, reduce prices and thus help the poor. (If the opportunity cost of allowances leads to price increases, these results would no hold.)

However, as noted, emissions trading programmes can create some additional transitional unemployment. The compensatory programmes for workers discussed above would be equally relevant for emissions trading programmes. There are, of course, the same concerns about effectiveness and targeting.

Chapter 7

Conclusions

Distributive impacts have been prominent elements in the policy debates surrounding the major actual or proposed economic incentive programmes. Discussions of a national carbon tax often focus on whether a national tax would hurt the poor, put coal miners out of work, or derail export industries. These considerations were key consideration in the design of the Swedish carbon tax and in the carbon tax proposal of the European Commission. Attempts to avoid economic dislocations by coordinating the tax globally run into concerns for impacts on developing countries.

Distributive issues have also been key elements for emissions trading programmes, although the issues tend to concern who gets the gains as well as who might be harmed. For example, the formula to allocate initial allowances was one of the most contentious issues in the debate over the acid rain provision of the 1990 Clean Air Act in the United States. A similar debate is going on in the Los Angeles Basin in California as that region develops a trading programme to deal with urban smog. Both small businesses and labour groups are concerned that the programme would hurt them. These concerns have lead to proposals to modify the programmes and avoid such losses.

A. Key functions of a distributive analysis

It is important to point out that all policies have distributive impacts. Some groups win and some may lose. A crucial element of economic instruments is, however, that they are not zero-sum games. Both emissions taxes and emissions trading programmes allow important environmental targets to be met more cheaply—and with greater assurance—than the traditional command-and-control system that dominates environmental regulation in OECD countries. This means that efforts should be made to design policies that achieve these ends while protecting legitimate distributive concerns.

Because determining the distributive impacts is complex, policy debates are often not based upon a formal distributive analysis. This can lead to misinformation (or incomplete information) that is destructive to the policy debate. For example, much of the concern with the Los Angeles trading programme is based upon speculation that the programme would harm small businesses. A distributive analysis clarifies how firms might gain or lose with trading—indicating the importance of the initial allocation—and shows that some of the concerns of small businesses are not justified.

Similar analyses of carbon taxes show how the impacts depend in large part on how revenues are handled and also point the way to modifications that might lessen any adverse impacts.

In short, a distributive analysis can be an important component of a full analysis of economic instruments. It can serve two principal functions:

1. A distributive analysis can clarify what is *actually* at stake for particular groups when economic instruments are used to deal with environmental problems.

2. A distributive analysis can point the way to *sensible* mitigation or compensation strategies.

These two objectives are related. Clarifying what is actually at stake is likely to show that in many cases efficiency and equity objectives are both served by economic instruments. That case is clearest for emissions trading programmes that grandfather allowances. If allowances are distributed to firms in the same way as under a command-and-control alternative, all firms (and eventually all consumers) share in the overall cost savings. Although some workers may become unemployed (at least temporarily), the majority of workers would gain as well.

B. Check list for distributive analysis

What analyses would be most useful? This study emphasizes the importance of the *framework* for performing a distributive analysis. It is possible to translate this framework into a checklist of questions or issues to be considered. The following are key elements of such a checklist.

1. What is the benchmark for comparison?

Determining the benchmark is a "threshold" issue on which there is no right or wrong answer. There are two principal alternatives: (1) the "no regulation" or independent case in which the incentive scheme is judged against the status quo; and (2) the comparative case in which the incentive scheme is compared to the impacts of an equivalent command-and-control alternative.

Most evaluations of emissions trading programmes take the comparative approach. For example, analyses of the United States acid rain trading programme illustrate how firms in various industries are affected by a *switch* from traditional controls that would achieve the same total emission reduction. In contrast, most studies of the incidence of carbon taxes implicitly assume an independent analysis. Regardless of the choice, however, it is important to be clear about the benchmark in performing the analysis and reporting results.

2. Will the economic instrument lead to government revenues?

Emissions tax and emissions trading programmes are similar in most respects. The major distinction in fact is not among the two versions but rather between emissions taxes and auctioned trading programmes, on the one hand, and grandfathered trading programmes. The latter do not lead to government revenues. While they are transfers from an overall societal perspective, government revenues have a major impact on the distributive consequences. It is therefore important to determine early in the analysis whether substantial revenues will be collected.

Whether a tax or trading programme will be evaluated will depend upon a host of institutional and other considerations. Tax policies appear to be considered more in European and Scandinavian countries, while marketable permits programmes are more often discussed in the United States and Canada. While this pattern probably reflects historical conditions (indirect taxes are a more integral part of European and Scandinavian tax systems), it may be useful to consider both approaches for some applications. Moreover, in some cases it may be useful to study a mixed approach in which economic instruments are combined with traditional regulations.

3. What are the initial impacts of economic instruments?

The framework here emphasizes the need to be clear about the initial impacts of economic incentive programmes. The initial impacts depend upon several choices regarding the nature of the analysis and the economic incentives, including most importantly the following:

- benchmark; and

- government revenues.

These decisions determine the initial impacts that are involved in the distributive analysis.

4. What are the relevant groups for which impacts will be addressed (either quantitatively or qualitatively)?

Distributive analyses done by economists typically focus on the costs borne by different income groups. This focus is in part a legacy of the heritage of tax incidence analysis, in which the degree of regressivity or progressivity is one of key evaluative criteria used to evaluate alternative taxes. Most analyses have also focused on long-term impacts, in which case transitional costs on labour (i.e., unemployment) are ignored.

The empirical case studies suggest that the list of relevant groups should be broadened. For example, concerns with the Los Angeles trading programme focused on the cost impacts on small businesses and the transitional impacts on workers. Similarly, much of the analyses of carbon taxes concerns gains and losses to industry or geographic groups.

5. What empirical steps are needed to determine the final impacts (taking into account the shifting of costs or benefits to other groups)?

All costs are eventually borne by individuals. Businesses and governments do not bear costs (although stockholders and taxpayers do). However, determining the costs that individuals bear requires estimating changes in business costs and government revenues.

The nature and structure of the economic incentive scheme will of course affect the analysis. It is possible, however, to lay out a series of steps for a typical distributional analysis that focuses on the long-term effects on income groups and the transitional impacts on workers. These steps are the following (this list assumes that the economic instrument leads to business cost increases, i.e., the "no regulation" benchmark):

1. Determine change in compliance costs (i.e., control costs plus any costs to pay taxes or purchase allowances) by industry.

2. Determine impacts of changes in compliance costs as well as the impacts of "opportunity costs" on product prices and output, by industry.

3. Determine impacts of price/output changes on "transitional costs" to workers in the relevant geographic groups (i.e., determine how many workers might become unemployed in the short-term due to output changes in the region).

4. Determine impacts of higher product prices on consumers in different income groups, based upon expenditure survey data.

5. Determine impacts of price and output changes on firm profits, by industry.

6. Determine the division of changes in firm profits between stockholders and taxpayers (in countries with corporate profits taxes).

7. Allocate the shareholder and taxpayer changes to income groups based upon survey data on their shares of corporate profits and income taxes, respectively.

8. If government revenues are collected, allocate them to income categories based upon the same survey data showing the share of income taxes paid by each income group. (Modify this step if the revenues are targeted to reduce specific taxes or to pay for new programmes.)

9. Sum the results of the price impacts, the shareholder impacts and the taxpayer impacts for each income group.

10. Summarize the results of the analyses for income groups, workers, and regions.Although this list contains a number of simplifying assumptions, it provides a useful structure.

6. What options are available to mitigate or compensate for any groups harmed by the use of economic instruments?

The analysis should include an investigation of the advantages and disadvantages of mitigation or compensation strategies. It is useful to distinguish these two mechanisms (mitigation is an *ex ante* concept while compensation refers to aiding groups *ex post*). Such an analysis would search for means of reducing adverse impacts without compromising the advantages of the programme or creating other problems.

C. Concluding remarks

Carbon taxes and other economic instruments are certain to be on the policy agenda of OECD countries for many years. Decisions on whether or not to adopt such policies will depend upon a large number of scientific, economic and political judgements.

It would be virtually impossible to avoid *all* losses from the use of economic instruments. Emissions taxes will hit some consumers harder than others, some industries harder than others, and some workers harder than others. Similarly, although emissions trading programmes are widely regarded as saving costs and reducing impacts relative to command and control standard, *some* groups will inevitably be worse off.

It does appear possible, however, to avoid the major redistributive difficulties from economic instruments. The income distribution impacts of emissions taxes can be compensated for by changes in the tax code. Initial allocation formulas for emissions trading programmes can be designed that allow the programmes to pass key political hurdles. Major employment dislocations can be dealt with through general transfer or retraining programmes. The net result of adding these mitigation or compensation elements would be economic incentive programmes that achieve *both* efficiency and equity objectives.

ENDNOTES

1. This study draws on several companion OECD efforts, including Albert (1991), de Savornin Lohman (1992), and ongoing studies being carried out by the Task Force on Taxation and the Environment and the program on the Socio-economic Aspects of Climate Change.

2. OECD (1989) identifies two other types of environmental charging schemes, administrative charges and tax differentiation. Administrative charges are charges for government services such as registration of chemicals or implementation of regulations. Tax differentiation leads to more favorable prices for "environmentally friendly" products, and is thus similar to product charges except that the tax differentiation option is usually not designed to raise net revenue.

3. Several authors have pointed out the importance of uncertainty about benefits and costs in determining whether a trading or a tax scheme is the preferred approach. For a theoretical treatment, see Weitzman (1974) or Nichols (1984). For empirical applications, see Harrison (1983) or Nichols (1983).

4. The literature on economic instruments (also referred to as economic incentives, market incentives and market-based approaches) is voluminous. Examples include Ackerman and Stewart (1988), Anderson et al. (1977), Dales (1968), Kneese and Schultze (1976), Schelling (1983), Stavins (1988), Stavins (1991), and Tietenberg (1985). The discussion in this section draws on Harrison and Nichols (1990b).

5. This example assumes that the plants do not own any rights to emit pollutant, and thus that both Plant I and Plant II would purchase the right to emit a ton under the emissions trading scheme. The savings in control cost would be the same if Plant I were assumed to be able to sell the right emit the additional ton it controlled. As noted below, however, the overall impacts—including payments to the government—would differ depending upon the state of initial property rights.

6. This conclusion ignores some complications based on how the revenues are used. Transferring revenues to the government could lead to net gains if more distorting taxes were reduced (see Terkla 1984 and Repetto et al. 1992). In contrast, the transfer could lead to a net loss if the government funded relatively inefficient programs with the added revenues (see Harrison 1983).

7. For a more general analysis of the problem of selecting appropriate targets for incentives and standards, see Nichols (1984). As Nichols shows, the appropriate target often depends on the regulatory instrument to be used.

8. Additional information on experience with emissions trading in the United States is contained in Hahn and Hester (1989), Harrison and Nichols (1990b), Carlin (1992), and Tietenberg (1992).

9. See Kete (1992) for a discussion of other major provisions of the acid rain trading program and the political considerations surrounding its development.

10. The OECD is currently updating its 1989 study on the experience with economic incentives.

11. The benefits might differ if the location or timing of the emission reductions changes from one approach to the other. Because emissions can cause vastly different damages depending upon where and when they occur, a constant level of emissions does not guarantee a constant level of damages. (See Nichols 1984 for a theoretical treatment of these issues.) However, there is no reason on a priori grounds to expect the pattern of emissions to create more or less damage under an economic incentive approach. (See Nichols and Harrison 1990b, for an empirical case study in which changing to a trading program led to *more* air quality benefits.)

12. For analysis of the distributive effects on the benefit side, see Baumol and Oates (1988) and Harrison and Rubinfeld (1978b).

13. A shift in tax revenue can, however, affect overall economic efficiency as well. See Terkla (1984) and Shackleton et al. (1992) for discussions of the efficiency gains from environmental taxes.

14. In general these details do not affect the overall efficiency of the economic instrument. There is one major exception. The allocation formula under the "grandfathered" allowance approach can affect the efficiency of the result if the formula is tied to current or future behavior (e.g., a firm receives more allowances next year if its emissions are greater this year). See Harrison and Nichols (1990c) for a discussion of this issue.

15. See Musgrave and Musgrave (1984, Chapter 12) for a discussion of the difference between initial (or statutory) incidence and eventual incidence in the context of tax incidence.

16. This section draws heavily on Nichols and Harrison (1991) and Harrison and Nichols (1992a).

17. See Harrison et al. (1992) for an application of this benefit assessment methodology to air pollution in the Los Angeles air basin.

18. Since standards are typically written in terms of emissions per unit of output or input (e.g., pounds of NO_x per Btu for electric utilities), command-and-control regulations do not actually impose a limitation on mass emissions sources. For example, a power plant could meet a limit of 0.2 pounds of NO_x per million Btu with vastly different overall emissions depending upon its capacity utilization. Allocations under allowance trading, in contrast, *would* limit total emissions. This feature of a trading program provides greater certainty that air quality standards would be met and thus represents an environmental advantage of the emissions trading approach.

19. The net impacts of the price change can also be very different for different firms in the same industry. Firms whose costs decline more than the price decrease will, on net, be better off (see Leone and Jackson 1981). This suggests, again, that the more a firm's control costs differ from the norm, *in either direction*, the better off it will be in a switch from command-and-control to economic instruments.

20. The following review is not exhaustive. However, the studies reviewed in this section are representative of the empirical information in this area.

Appendix

Distributive Impacts of the Los Angeles Basin Emissions Trading Programme

The emissions trading plan being developed in the Los Angeles air basin provides a good opportunity to show how distributive analyses can be useful as economic instruments move from theory to practice. Distributive issues have been key elements of the public debate over the programme.

A. Background

The Los Angeles basin emissions trading programme is named the Regional Clean Air Incentives Market, or RECLAIM, to emphasize the possibility of using economic instruments to reclaim both clean air and a healthy economy. On March 5, 1992, the Governing Board of the South Coast Air Quality Management District (SCAQMD) authorized its staff to develop specific rules to implement RECLAIM.

1. Overview of RECLAIM

RECLAIM represents a major departure from the traditional command-and-control approach that has been used to regulate air pollution in the Los Angeles basin. The two key elements of RECLAIM are:

- a cap on emissions from sources covered by the programme that declines over time, so that by 2010 federal air quality standards are projected to be met; and

- the authority given sources to trade emissions reduction credits among one another.

The RECLAIM programme is different from previous trading programmes primarily because of its potential breadth. RECLAIM initially would replace as many as 62 present and future command-and-control regulations governing emissions of reactive organic gasses (ROG), nitrogen oxides (NO_x) and sulfur oxides (SO_x) from large stationary sources (sources greater than or equal to 4 tons of emissions per year). This will create a ROG trading market of about 2,000 facilities, a NO_x market of about 700 facilities, and an SO_x market of about 70 facilities. These facilities include a wide variety of industrial and commercial sources. SCAQMD officials envision expanding the market to include additional stationary sources, mobile sources, and area sources. Such a programme would be much more extensive than current trading programmes, including the United States acid rain trading programme for electric utilities contained in the 1990 Clean Air Act. (See South Coast Air Quality Management District 1992 for a detailed discussion of the elements of RECLAIM.) The United States Environmental Protection Agency has indicated that RECLAIM might function as a model for similar trading programmes in other polluted urban regions of the United States.

The RECLAIM programme was the result of a nine-month long feasibility study conducted by SCAQMD staff with input provided by Advisory and Steering Committees set up by the SCAQMD.[1] The SCAQMD feasibility study was preceded by two studies presented to the public at a workshop organized by the SCAQMD (Harrison and Nichols 1990a and Noll 1990). The SCAQMD feasibility study resulted in five Working Papers as well as a report presenting summary recommendations and an economic evaluation of the plan (South Coast Air Quality Management District 1992). Comments on these Working Papers and the specific elements of RECLAIM were submitted by members of the Advisory and Steering Committees and from many other parties, including the Regulatory Flexibility Group (Wyman 1991), a coalition of Southern California businesses and associations, and the Coalition for Clean Air (Schwartz 1992). In sum, there has been a great deal of discussion and evaluation of RECLAIM.

Virtually everyone agrees that the programme has the potential to lower the cost of meeting ambitious air quality targets. Some public commentators and members of the Advisory Committee, however, raised questions about the distribution impacts of RECLAIM. Two main concerns were raised. First, small business representatives argued that they would be harmed by the programme and that all the gains would be reaped by big businesses, which were the most vocal supporters of the programme. Second, labour representatives argued that the programme would put people out of work because the possibility of "shut down credits" would create incentives to close factories.

2. Overview of this appendix

RECLAIM is a complex programme that will have a major impact on virtually all firms and households in the Los Angeles Basin. Complete data are not available to estimate all of the distributive impacts. However, it is possible to provide empirical information on four key distributive questions raised by the programme:

- How does the formula used to distribute initial allowances influence the gains to various participants in RECLAIM?

- Will RECLAIM harm small businesses?

- What effect will RECLAIM have on overall employment in the Los Angeles region?

- What policy options are available to mitigate or compensate for any negative job impacts of RECLAIM?

A major purpose of this Appendix is to address each of these issues, using available empirical evidence.[2] In addition, the Appendix is intended to illustrate how a distributive analysis can be undertaken using the framework outlined in this study.

120

The Appendix is organized as follows. The following section addresses the threshold issues outlined in the study in order to provide the necessary structure for the distributive analysis. Information on the potential cost savings are then presented, including a discussion of the implications of these results for households in different income groups in the Los Angeles air basin. The following four sections address the four distributive issues listed above. A conceptual analysis is used to illustrate the importance of the allocation formula. Small business impacts are evaluated using a detailed case study of how one industry (furniture manufacturers) are affected by RECLAIM. The impacts of RECLAIM on employment and the evaluations of various mitigation and compensation strategies are evaluated using conceptual formulations. The Appendix concludes with a summary of results.

B. Threshold issues

The structure outlined in Chapter 3 of this study can be used to clarify the nature of the distributive analysis of RECLAIM.

1. *Benchmark.* The benchmark is the set of command-and-control regulations that would achieve the same emissions reductions as RECLAIM. That means that benefits are *not* part of the analysis and that the initial impact on businesses is to *reduce* overall control costs.

2. *Government revenues.* RECLAIM is based upon grandfathering allowances, and thus *no* additional government revenues are collected. (The formula for initially allocating allowances is, however, one of the key items in the distributive analysis.)

3. *Initial and final incidence.* One of the key issues in the policy discussions concerns the impacts of RECLAIM on different industry groups, particularly small businesses. Final impacts on different income groups are also of concern, though less frequently discussed.

4. *Transitional impacts.* There was great interest in the potential impacts of RECLAIM on workers. In particular, labour leaders were concerned that the use of "shut-down credits" would lead firms to close operations in the Basin.

5. *Relevant groups.* As mentioned, key groups of interest in the policy debate are different industries (particularly small businesses) and workers. (Income distributional impacts were not emphasized, but they are discussed here as well.)

6. *Modeling technique.* The impacts on business costs from RECLAIM are based upon microeconomic modeling of the results of trading.

C. Potential cost savings

1. How RECLAIM can lower compliance costs

It is useful to summarize the major cost-saving opportunities created by RECLAIM, based on various opportunities for trading:

- allowing trading *within* a facility will reallocate emissions reductions from relatively high-cost to relatively low-cost options (e.g., a furniture manufacturer could shift controls from one emission source to another within its facility);

- allowing trading between facilities in the *same industry* (or source category) yields even greater savings (e.g., two furniture manufacturers could trade to reduce their overall cost);

- allowing trading between facilities in *different industries* extends the cost savings (e.g., further reductions by furniture manufacturers could result in avoiding extraordinarily expensive new controls on refineries);

- focusing on *mass emissions reductions* rather than on controlling emissions *rates* makes available additional cost-effective control options (e.g., utilities would be encouraged to use fuel conservation as a method of reducing emissions); and

- creating a market price for emission allowances would provide greater incentives for *technological innovation* that could substantially reduce future control costs as well as improve future air quality.

All of these mechanisms have the effect of giving firms greater flexibility to meet given emissions targets.

2. Ilustrative savings within source categories

The following results provide an indication of the likely cost savings from instituting RECLAIM and thus shed light on the size of the gains that might be shared among various participants in the market. These estimates are based upon information provided by the SCAQMD on the cost of reducing NO_x emissions.

a) Electric utility boilers

The SCAQMD identified 54 active utility boilers to which emission rules would apply. For each, it estimated the costs of complying with three different standards. These data were used to estimate the costs of achieving the various standards, and the costs of achieving equivalent reductions in NO_x emissions using emissions trading. Figure A-1 plots the results of these analyses. The horizontal axis shows total emission reductions, while the vertical axis measures costs. The three potential standards are plotted as individual points connected by lines. The bottom curve shows the minimum cost of achieving any given level of emission reductions; it was constructed by ranking the various plant-control combinations in ascending order of their incremental cost per ton reduced.

Figure A-1. **Cost savings to electric utility boilers under trading**

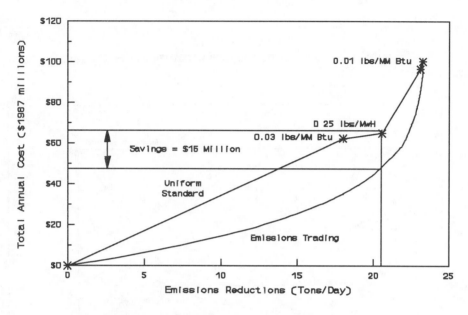

Source: Harrison and Nichols 1990c, p. 65

Note that the least-cost line lies well below the points representing the individual standards; i.e., substantial cost savings could be reaped with trading. For the intermediate standard—0.25 lbs/MWHr—trading would reduce the cost by about 25 percent compared to that of a uniform standard. The cost savings, of course, depend upon the level of the emission standard; savings from trading would be about 43 percent if the standard were set at the lowest level.

The trading programme reduces costs because of the very large differences among boilers in the cost of controls. Among the entire group of 54 boilers, the average cost ranges from $3,000 per ton to more than $130,000 per ton.

b) Cogenerators

A similar analysis was performed for NO_x controls on stationary gas turbines, used mostly for cogeneration. Cost and emission data were available for two different control levels: 42 parts per million (ppm) and 9 ppm. Figure A-2 plots the costs for the two control levels on the assumption that they would apply to all sources, as well as a "mixed" standard in which the standard of 42 ppm would apply to units less than 2.9 MW and the 9 ppm standard would apply to larger units. The figure also shows the least-cost means of achieving increasingly large emissions reductions. These results show that a trading scheme would save about 23 percent of the costs of achieving the same emission reductions as the "mixed" standard.

Figure A-2. Cost savings to cogenerators under trading

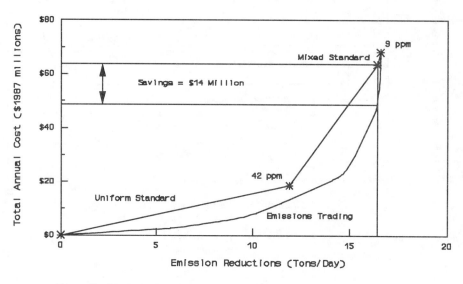

Source: Harrison and Nichols 1990c, p 67

3. Cost savings from RECLAIM

The SCAQMD has developed cost options for a total of 50 of the source categories that would be covered by RECLAIM. The costs are based on control options in the 1991 Air Quality Management Plan (see South Coast Air Quality Management District 1991b). Figure A-3 shows the SCAQMD estimates of the average reduction cost per ton of ROG for these 50 source categories. The average reduction cost per ton of ROG ranges from $113 per ton to $86,970 per ton.

Figure A-3. SCAQMD cost data shows wide differences in average reduction cost per ton of ROG among source categories

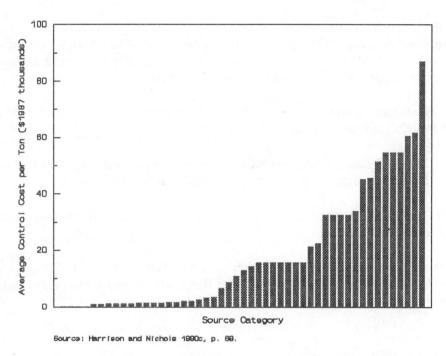

Source: Harrison and Nichols 1990c, p. 69.

Figure A-4. RECLAIM Lowers Overall Control Costs

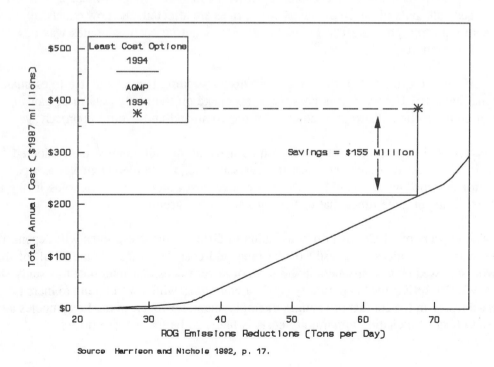

Source Harrison and Nichols 1992, p. 17.

This wide variation in cost per ton suggests that overall costs could be reduced substantially by trading. The general methodology developed for electric power plants can be used to create a "least-cost" supply curve for emissions reductions from these data.

Figure A-4 shows the "least-cost" supply curve for all of the source categories for which SCAQMD data are available. The figure also shows the total cost and emissions reductions reported for the equivalent AQMP measures. These results suggest that a trading scheme would save about 40 percent of the costs of the command-and-control approach.[3]

This estimate is likely to be a substantial underestimate of the true cost savings from RECLAIM for two reasons:

1. These data do not take into account the variation in costs for individual sources *within* a source category (e.g., individual internal combustion engines).

2. These data only account for a relatively narrow trading programme, focused on large stationary sources.

If these limitations were relaxed, the estimated cost savings from RECLAIM could increase substantially. In sum, there seems little doubt that RECLAIM would lead to very large cost savings for firms in the Los Angeles basin.

4. Income distributional impacts

The pattern of gains to households in different income groups will depend upon which industries receive the bulk of the cost savings, how prices are affected, and how expenditure patterns compare across income groups. The methodology for preparing such estimates was described in Chapter 4 of this report.

Sufficient information on the effects of emission trading is not available to estimate these distributional impacts. However, it is possible to speculate on the likely pattern of gains by using information on the income distribution impacts of the command-and-control approach.

Figure A-5 shows the estimated cost burdens of the air quality plan adopted by the SCAQMD in 1989.[4] As expected, the costs are regressive; i.e., the burden is greater as a percentage of income for low income households. The percentage cost burden for households in the lowest income group is about three times that of the highest income group.[5]

The impacts of RECLAIM on households in different income groups will depend largely upon what happens to prices as a result of the predicted cost decreases. Some or all of the cost savings will be passed on to consumers in the form of lower prices. Chapter 4 of this study showed that prices will also reflect the "opportunity cost" of emissions, which would tend to increase prices. As discussed below in the context of changes in employment, however, in the Los Angeles air basin the long-run effect of including opportunity costs is likely to be to decrease prices.

Figure A-5. **Cost Savings Due to RECLAIM are Particularly Important to Lower Income Households**

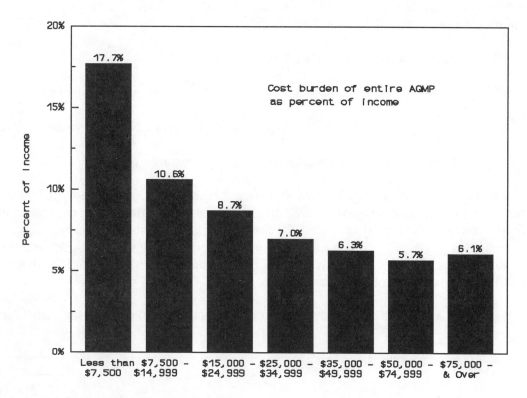

Source: Harrison and Nichols 1992, p. 25.

RECLAIM would therefore work to the advantage of lower income groups in the long run. Because they bear a disproportionate share of the costs of the command-and-control approach, lower income households would reap a disproportionate share of the gains from cost reductions. Rather than representing a tradeoff between equity and efficiency, therefore, RECLAIM illustrates how these two goals can be complementary.

D. Influence of allocation formula on firm and industry costs

The conceptual foundation given in Chapter 4 of this study showed that the size of the cost savings to a particular firm or industry depends on the following three major factors:

1. The price of allowances.

2. The firm or industry's costs relative to the allowance price.

3. The firm or industry's allocation of allowances.

127

The first two factors could lead to smaller *gains* to a firm or industry but they would not account for an industry facing higher costs with RECLAIM. In contrast, changes in the allocation can lead to greater compliance costs with RECLAIM than under the AQMP. This section shows that the determination of a "fair" allocation formula can be very complex.

1. Allocation of allowances under RECLAIM

The allocation formula proposed for RECLAIM consists of two principal elements:

1. The "baseline" allocation received in the first year of the programme (1994).

2. The rate at which its number of allowances declines over time.

RECLAIM establishes a 1994 baseline allocation for each emission source by reducing actual or permitted emissions as reported in 1987 by 30 percent, reflecting an average annual decline of approximately 5 percent as mandated for the overall basin in state legislation. These baseline allocations would be reduced by a fixed rate for all participants. Figure A-6 illustrates this allocation formula. (The figure is illustrative and not based upon the specific time paths proposed in RECLAIM, which differ for NO_x and ROG.)

Figure A-6. **RECLAIM provides a uniform decline in allowances for each source**

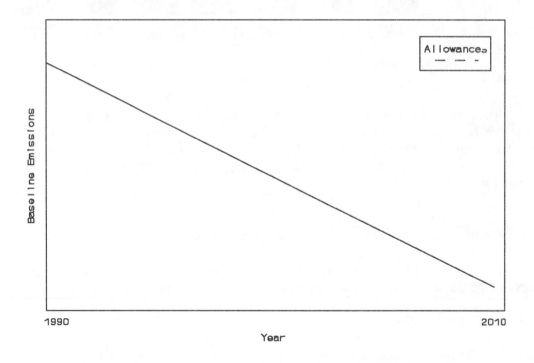

Is this allowance allocation approach fair? There is of course no single definition of "fairness." In addressing this question, the following issues have been raised.

a) Prior controls

Calculating the allocation using actual or permitted emissions in 1987 is considered unfair by firms that have invested in substantial control before that date. Figure A-7 illustrates this issue for two hypothetical industries. Both industries have the same emissions in 1987, and thus both would receive the same first-year allocation under RECLAIM.

The two differ significantly, however, in how they reach that common point. Industry A has controlled its emissions by 75 percent in the early 1980's in response to SCAQMD requirements. Industry B has not been subject to requirements and thus has not controlled in the past.

Figure A-7. **Allocations under RECLAIM do not consider prior controls**

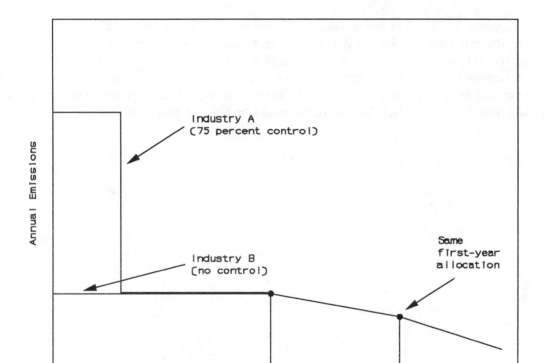

An alternative is to base the first-year baseline on "uncontrolled" emissions. This approach would have the effect of rewarding those industries that have controlled substantially in the past and penalizing industries that have not controlled before. Whether that change would be more or less fair is a matter of opinion. However, determining the level of "uncontrolled" emissions is likely to prove very difficult in practice.

b) Fluctuations in actual emissions

Another issue involves the use of a single year (1987) as the basis for the first-year allocation. Industries (or firms) whose emissions were abnormally low in 1987 naturally would object to that single year being chosen. Figure A-8 illustrates this difficulty for an industry with fluctuating emissions that happen to be low in 1987.

One solution for this problem would be to use the highest year or an average of several years to calculate an industry's share of the total 1993 allowances. For example, Wyman (1991) recommends using the highest annual actual emissions within the five-year period from 1987 to 1991 as the basis for the first-year allocation.

c) Offsets for post-1976 equipment

Equipment placed in service after 1976 in the Los Angeles basin has been subject to new source review programmes. Part of the new source review was a requirement to offset emissions, either by reducing emissions elsewhere in the facility or by purchasing offsets from other sources. These reductions led to emission reduction credits (ERCs) in cases where the offsets were greater than the emissions from the new source. The allowance levels for these pieces of equipment were set to take into account the fact that emissions would be reduced elsewhere.

Figure A-8. **Allocations under RECLAIM would be based on emissions in a single year**

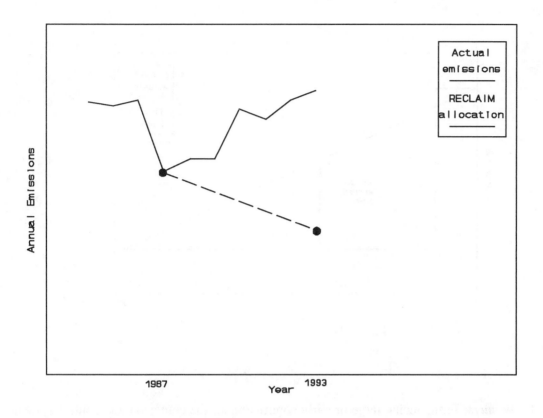

The argument for crediting industries with their ERCs and using permitted rather than actual emissions for post-1976 equipment is similar to that for taking into account prior controls—these additional control measures reflect a prior contribution to clean air that should be recognized when allowances are allocated.[6]

2. *Contrast between allocation under RECLAIM and under command-and-control alternative*

Perhaps the most basic characteristic of the allocation formula proposed for RECLAIM is that it is very *different* than that under the alternative command-and-control approach. While RECLAIM would create a uniform decline for all sources, the command-and-control system results in enormous variations among sources in the emissions that are allowed.

This difference in treatment of future emissions allowances arises from the same factors that lead to differences in prior control: there is an enormous difference in *when* emission standards are set for different industries.

These differences in the timing of the command-and-control regulations can create large impacts on costs to different firms from switching to the uniform RECLAIM system. Figures A-9 and Figure A-10 illustrate the two extreme cases:

131

Figure A-9. "Winners" include firms with large or early controls under AQMP

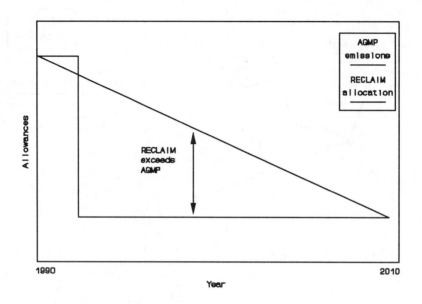

1. *Winners*. Firms facing large or early controls under the command-and-control system would gain with RECLAIM.

2. *Losers*. Firms with small or late controls under the command-and-control system *may* lose with RECLAIM.

Is the pattern of winners and losers fair? As with the allocation of first-year allowances, there is no single measure of fairness. However, there are several points to keep in mind as one evaluates these patterns:

- the pattern of emission reductions under the command-and-control approach does not have any particular claim to being the "correct" one;

- "losers" in one year (e.g., 1997) can easily become "winners" later on (e.g., 2000) because of the timing of the AQMP controls; and

- cost savings to "losers" can easily overwhelm the "losses" from fewer benchmark allocations.

- attempting to "fine tune" the allocation of allowances to deal with "equity issues" could bog RECLAIM down in conflicts that might undermine the basic workings of the programme; and

132

Figure A-10. "Losers" include firms with small or late controls under AQMP

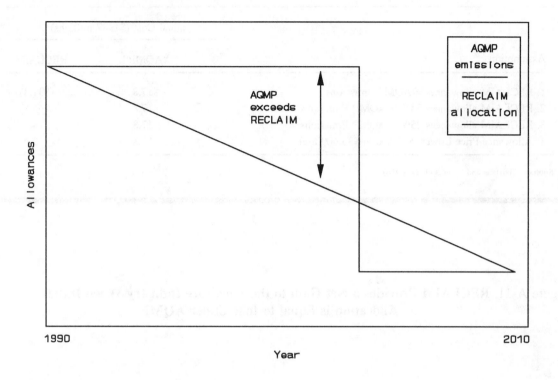

• using the AQMP emissions as a guide would have the advantage of guaranteeing that all firms and industries would be "winners" under RECLAIM.

E. Case study of cost impacts: furniture manufacturing industry

It is useful to illustrate the way in which an industry's costs are affected by trading options under RECLAIM—and by the allocation formula—by estimating results for a specific industry. This section presents results for the furniture manufacturing industry, using the SCAQMD cost data.[7] Table A-1 gives the results of simulating the cost to the furniture industry under both the command-and-control system and RECLAIM, under several different sets of assumptions.

1. RECLAIM allocation equals that under command-and-control

The first row of Table A-1 gives the results under the assumption that the industry's initial allocation under RECLAIM is equal to that under the command-and-control programme; Figure A-11 shows the two costs graphically. The difference is dramatic. Control costs are estimated to be about $18 million under the command-and-control regulations. In contrast, the industry is estimated to receive *net revenues* of $31 million under RECLAIM, i.e., overall, the furniture industry's revenues from the sale of allowances would substantially exceed its control costs.

Table A-I. **Cost to furniture industry under alternative assumptions regarding RECLAIM**

	Annual Cost ($1987 millions)	
Assumption	"AQMP"	RECLAIM
1. RECLAIM allowances = AQMP Emissions	$17.8	($31.3)
2. RECLAIM allowances 25% > AQMP Emissions	17.8	(66.8)
3. RECLAIM allowances 25% < AQMP Emissions	17.8	4.1
4. Allowance Price Lower ($17,600 v. $33,600/ton)	17.8	2.2

Source: Harrison and Nichols (1992, p. 58).

Figure A-11. **RECLAIM Provides a Net Gain to the Furniture Industry When Initial Allocation is Equal to that Under AQMP**

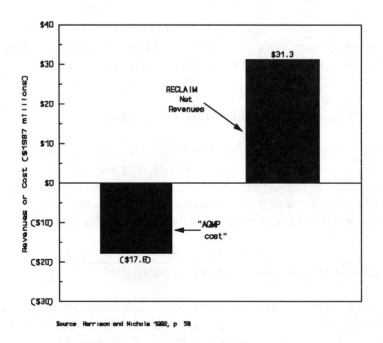

Figure A-12 shows why the furniture manufacturers do so well under trading. That figure shows the marginal cost curve for emissions reductions for the industry as well as the estimated price at which emissions would trade. According to the SCAQMD cost data, furniture manufacturers have many options to control emissions at costs substantially below the projected allowance price. The shaded area shows the profit the industry makes from the sale of emissions allowances in excess of those it would be allocated under the command-and-control system.

Figure A-12. **Cost savings to furniture industry under RECLAIM**

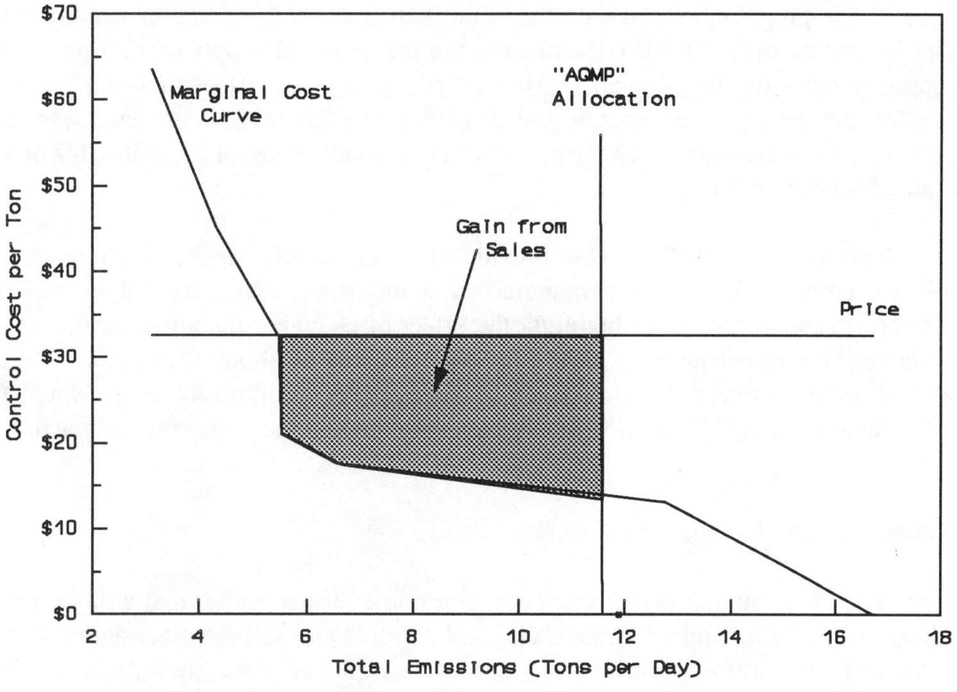

Source: Harrison and Nichols 1992.

2. Emission allocation differs from command-and-control

The second and third rows of Table A-1 show the effects of changing the allocation of allowances. If furniture manufacturers were allocated 25 percent *more* emission allowances under RECLAIM than under traditional controls, their net revenues would increase from $31 million to almost $67 million. In contrast, if they were allocated 25 percent *fewer* allowances, the situation would change dramatically. Rather than obtain net revenues of $31 million, the industry would incur net costs of about $4 million. Note, however, that even with 25 percent fewer allowances, the industry's costs would still be less than one-quarter of their costs under the command-and-control approach.

135

This simulation illustrates the proposition that focusing only on relative allowance allocations can be misleading. Industries can gain from emissions trading even if they receive fewer allowances than under the regulatory approach.

3. Allowance price changes

The gains to the furniture manufacturing industry under RECLAIM in this simulation are due both to the industry's low-cost control options and to the high allowance price (about $34,000 in 1997 based upon the SCAQMD data). This high price is due in part to the relatively small universe of the programme. One of the options in rule implementation would be to expand the number of sources in RECLAIM, thus increasing the potential supply of emission reduction credits and possibly reducing the allowance price.[8] To simulate the effect of lower control costs and a lower allowance price, the number of tons available for each control cost level was doubled and the resulting price was calculated. The result was an allowance price for ROG in 1997 of $17,600, about one-half of the original level.

The last row in Table A-I provides the results of using this alternative price on the compliance costs to the furniture manufacturing industry. (This simulation assumes allowance allocations are equal in order to highlight the effect of changing the allowance price.) Compliance costs change from a net revenue of $31 million to a cost of about $2 million. Thus, even with a reduced allowance price, net sellers (such as those in the furniture industry) would face far lower compliance costs under RECLAIM than under the command-and-control approach.

4. Summary of the furniture case study

The furniture industry is an example of a low-cost complier that will gain from the ability to reduce further than required under traditional controls and sell the allowances at a profit. Under the command-and-control approach, the industry's compliance costs are estimated to be roughly $18 million per year. The gains from trading are of course greater the more allowances the industry is allocated. When the allocation equals that under the regulatory approach, the profits from the sale of allowances result in net *revenues* of $31 million under RECLAIM. Even if the number of allowances were reduced to equal 75 percent of the AQMP allocation, the industry would face costs of only about $4 million, or only 23 percent of the $18 million cost under the command-and-control approach.

Other industries would gain from the opportunity to avoid high compliance costs through purchases from the furniture industry. Indeed, sales of allowances by the furniture industry mean that some high-cost complier is gaining. Any buyer would pay less to buy the allowances from furniture manufacturers than it would cost to control its own emissions. The only firms or industries that might lose are those whose RECLAIM allowances are substantially less than their allowable emissions under the command-and-control approach.

F. Assessing RECLAIM'S effect on employment

RECLAIM will affect employment in the Los Angeles air basin in several ways. The following are the major influences:[9]

1. Cost savings from RECLAIM will decrease prices and increase output.

2. "Opportunity cost" of emissions under RECLAIM will increase prices and decrease output.

3. Removal of the "new source bias" implicit in the regulatory approach will lead to long-term decreases in prices and increases in output.

1. Impact of cost savings

Lower control costs mean increased Basin production and increased Basin employment. Figure A-13 shows how RECLAIM would lower costs and increase output (and employment) for firms operating in the Basin.[10] The supply curve S_0 represents the initial conditions under the AQMP. The supply curve slopes up (firms will supply more if the price rises) based upon the firms' marginal costs of production, i.e., how much it costs to produce another unit of output. The demand curve reflects the fact that Basin consumers will demand more when the price declines. Under the AQMP, the equilibrium output is Q_0. With the cost savings from RECLAIM, the supply curve shifts out to S_1, leading to a new equilibrium at Q_1. These lower prices are translated into lower prices and expanded output. The expanded output increases the firms' demand for labour, which leads to long-term increases in Basin employment.

Figure A-13. Cost Savings from RECLAIM Lead to Greater Output and Greater Employment in the Basin

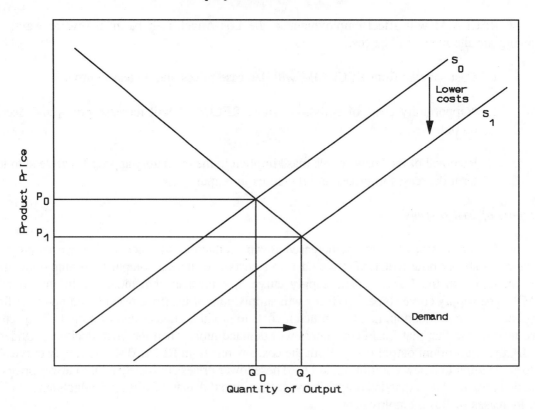

2. Impact of opportunity cost of allowances

The generally positive impacts of RECLAIM on employees must be tempered by the fact that emissions trading means that firms must consider the "opportunity cost" of emissions in a way that they do not with standards set under the AQMP. These opportunity costs will tend to at least partly offset the impacts of lower costs on output and employment at existing facilities. (As discussed in the following section, this effect is short-term; in the long-term, the relative treatment of *new sources* between RECLAIM and the AQMP would dominate.)

To understand these opportunity costs, consider the situation facing a company operating an existing facility that emits pollution. Under an emission standard such as those in the AQMP, the emissions that fall within the existing rules are "free" from the firm's perspective. It pays nothing for them nor would it receive any gain from reducing them. With trading under RECLAIM, however, those emissions are no longer free, because if they were eliminated, the allowances could be sold to another firm that wished to expand its operations or to reduce its need for more controls. Thus, in figuring the marginal cost of producing more output from the plant, the company must include an opportunity cost for the allowances needed. That opportunity cost will shift the supply curve inward.

138

Figure A-14 illustrates this effect. As in Figure A-13, the supply curve with the AQMP standards is indicated as S_0, while the impact of the cost savings with trading under RECLAIM is shown as S_1. If the opportunity cost of the cost savings is less than the cost savings—as shown by the curve S_2—the inward shift will not offset the gain shown earlier; the net increase in production and employment of RECLAIM would be reduced, but not reversed. However, if the opportunity cost is large relative to the cost savings, the net effect can be reversed. This case is shown as S_3 in Figure A-14.

Figure A-14. The Net Impact of RECLAIM Depends on the Size of Opportunity Costs of Allowances Relative to Cost Savings

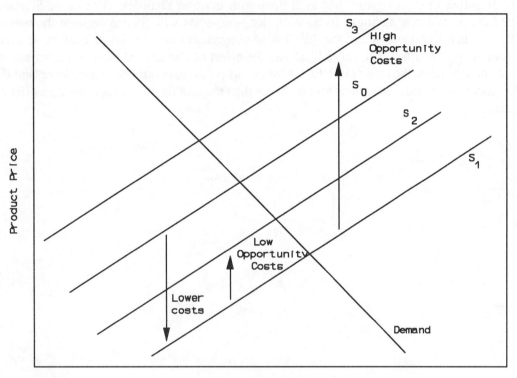

3. Impact of removal of the "New Source Bias"

The potential negative effect of opportunity costs on output and employment does *not* arise with new facilities, because the offset requirement now imposed with standards means that new facilities already must bear the cost of residual emissions.[11] Thus, even now new facilities will not be built unless the price received for output is high enough to cover the cost of buying offsets (as well as the cost of building the basic plant and meeting the very strict new-source emission standards).

The RECLAIM programme is likely to make it less costly to build new facilities. Because of the greater flexibility and the more developed market under the RECLAIM programme compared to the current offset programme, the effective price of allowances is likely to be lower than that for traditional offsets (including the high transactions costs associated with finding a willing seller and proving that a valid offset has been obtained.)

In the longer run, as existing plants retire and newer plants come to determine price and output levels, the effects of RECLAIM should be beneficial in virtually all markets. Figure A-15 illustrates the long-run situation when new sources dominate supply conditions. The supply curve with the new source standards is indicated as S_0^L (with the superscript "L" indicating that these relate to long-run conditions). The savings in control costs with RECLAIM will lower the costs and lead to greater output in the long-run, just as it does with existing facilities. The curve S_1^L shows the effect of the control cost savings. In addition, long-run costs will decline because the opportunity cost for residual emissions under the RECLAIM programme will be lower than those under the current offset programme. The curve S_2^L shows the effect of this second effect on costs and output. Thus, for new sources, the effects of RECLAIM are all positive; control costs are lower, and the cost of allowances for residual emissions will be lower than the cost of offsets required under the AQMP approach.

Figure A-15. **In the long-run RECLAIM will increase output**

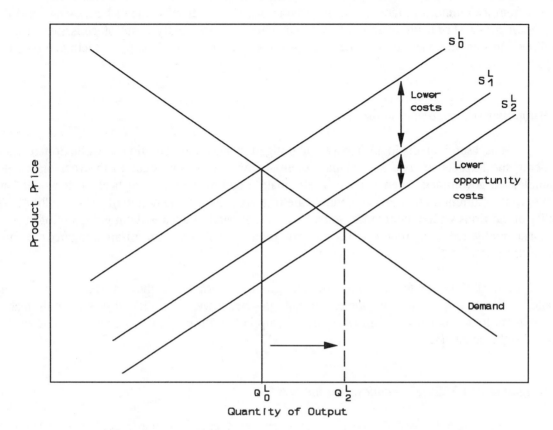

Creating an opportunity cost for residual emissions from existing sources—and thereby removing the current bias in favour of existing plants—may, however, accelerate the replacement of *some* existing facilities. This change will cause some worker dislocations and unemployment in situations in which the opportunity cost of allowances exceeds the cost savings from trading. How significant such short-term effects might be is an empirical question.

G. Policy options to reduce negative employment impacts

The previous section showed that any negative effects of RECLAIM on employment in the Los Angeles Basin are likely to result from the closing of *existing* facilities. The fact that existing facilities close does not, however, mean that *overall* production or employment in the industry would decline. Closing of existing facilities may simply be paving the way for new facilities when the "new source bias" is removed.

141

Nevertheless, the closing of existing facilities may lead to job losses in some sectors. New plants may require fewer workers. Plants in some sectors have not been subject to the "new source bias"—because they were not subject to stringent new source controls or because they received offsets from a Community Bank set up to provide offsets "for free" to small businesses—and thus the sector might shrink production when faced with the opportunity costs of emissions from its facilities. In sum, there are likely to be reasons to consider policy options for reducing employment impacts.

1. Mitigation versus compensation

It is useful to distinguish between mitigation and compensation. Mitigation refers to reducing the impacts *ex ante* so that the potential impacts do not occur in the first place. For example, the government might reduce or eliminate a control requirement because it would harm some group. Current environmental controls are often based on some notion of "affordability"—the ability of the firms within the industry to pay for control requirements without going out of business or substantially reducing production. Control requirements are thus often mitigated to avoid employment impacts.

Compensation refers to aid to particular groups *ex post* so that they are at least partly "made whole." For example, the government might go ahead with a policy it knows will lead to employment losses, but it would provide income support and training programmes to ease workers back into the economy.

2. Mitigation of RECLAIM employment impacts

There are a number of ways in which the adverse employment effects of RECLAIM might be prevented. However, these mitigation strategies tend to compromise RECLAIM's ability to lower the administrative and compliance costs of achieving emissions targets.

a) Change the initial allocation formula

The formula under RECLAIM is based upon allocating a *fixed* total number of emissions allowances each year. It is this cap on emissions that creates the opportunity cost of a plant's residual emissions. The fixed cap must be allocated to various sources (or other parties) on some basis that does not depend upon firms' current or future production or emission levels. If the allocation formula were based upon current or future activity, the cap would not be binding and no opportunity cost would be created for a plant's emissions.

Employment impacts from RECLAIM (relative to the equivalent AQMP measures) thus could be reduced or eliminated if the allocation formula were based upon current activity (production or emissions). A firm would then receive more initial allowances if it expanded production. No opportunity cost would be created. As a result, output and employment would tend to expand as a result of the cost savings from trading.

Although this policy would reduce employment impacts, it would also reduce the gains from RECLAIM. Firms would not have the proper incentives to decide whether or not to expand production in the Basin in light of the damages caused by their emissions. As a result, the overall cost of meeting emission reduction targets would increase.

How much would costs increase if the allocation formula were changed? It is impossible to tell without doing an empirical analysis. But it seems likely that the costs of meeting the *final* target (approximately an 85 percent decline in emissions) would increase substantially. Reducing production levels for highly polluting sources is likely to be a cost-effective option for reducing some emissions in the Basin. Removing those incentives would mean putting all of the pressure on technological solutions, which are likely to become very expensive as the reduction target is ratcheted down.

b) Disallow "shutdown credits"

Labour groups and others have proposed that firms not receive emission reduction credits when they shut down their plants. This policy could be accomplished by having firms forfeit their right to allowances if they close their facility. Such a policy would remove any incentive firms have to close their plants in order to sell emission allowances.

The disallowance of "shutdown credits" appears both to protect workers' jobs and to constitute a fair allocation formula. Why continue to give allowances to firms that no longer "need" them? However, the policy has two major shortcomings.

First, the policy would be very difficult to enforce because firms could so easily evade it. A firm could simply keep a skeleton crew working to avoid losing its allocation. Moreover, the implementation of the policy would present tough choices. Should a firm lose all its allowances if it shuts down its plant but also builds another to replace it? What if it uses the proceeds to invest in a completely different enterprise? Many of these same issues have plagued the current Federal programme for new source review, which has had to wrestle with thorny problems of determining when a plant is "new" and thus subject to more stringent emission standards. Enormous resources have been devoted to debates about whether modifications in a plant are so substantial as to constitute a new source and thus trigger review. Like this problem, the net result of requiring forfeiture of "shut down credits" is likely to be substantial legal maneuvering and increasing regulatory complexity. The "all-or-nothing" quality of the solution—the firm either retains all its scheduled allowances or forfeits them all—suggests that the incentives to evade the penalty would be substantial. The policy is therefore likely to lead to few changes in the employment impacts of the RECLAIM programme.

Second, even if it were successful, disallowing shutdown credits would remove appropriate incentives to modernize facilities and to reduce emissions by shifting to less polluting technologies. In effect, the disallowance would preserve and extend the current bias against new facilities that is inherent in more stringent emission standards for new facilities.

In sum, a simple programme to disallow "shutdown credits" would likely be ineffective and, to the extent that it did succeed at all, it would be a costly way of avoiding job losses.

c) Create non-transferable allowances

There is an intermediate ground between continuing to allocate allowances regardless of whether a plant is operating or not, on the one hand, and a "knife edge" solution in which a firm loses all of its allowances if it closes its plant, on the other. For example, a recent evaluation of emissions trading by the Canadian Council of Ministers of the Environment (cited by Nichols 1992) suggests distinguishing between two types of allowances, those that represent "current good practice" and those that cover any excess. The second category would not be transferable and thus would be forfeited if the plant shut down.

Figure A-16. **Forfeiture of "temporary" allowances when a plant shuts down**

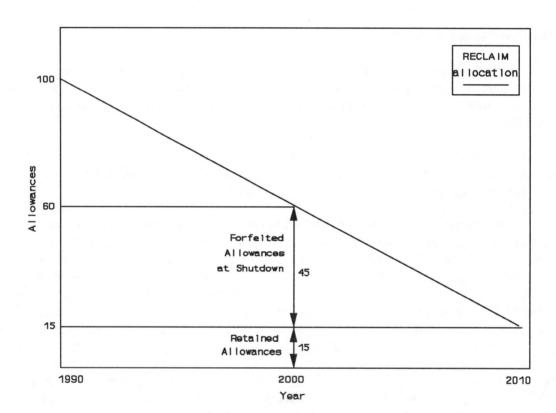

Figure A-16 illustrates how such a policy would work. A firm is assumed to receive an initial allowance for its one plant that begins at 100 tons in the first year and declines to 15 tons by the year 2010. The "permanent" allocation of 15 tons would be transferable and would be retained if the plant were closed down. However, the "temporary" allowances above 15 tons would be forfeited if the firm shut down. For example, if the plant were closed in the year 2000, the firm would forfeit allowances equal to 45 tons according to the schedule illustrated in Figure A-16.

144

This compromise programme, however, shares the same difficulties as the more extreme version discussed above in which *all* allowances would be forfeited. Firms would still have strong incentives to keep skeleton crews in their plants to avoid forfeiting allowances. The government would still face difficult decisions about whether a plant were "shut down" rather than replaced or modified. The net effects are likely to be substantial administrative complexity, greater transactions costs, and probably relatively little effect on Basin employment.

3. Compensation programmes

There are a number of ways to target compensation to those put out of work as a result of the RECLAIM programme. On balance, however, it may be more equitable to upgrade general unemployment support and retraining programmes rather than to target those affected by RECLAIM for special assistance.

a) Target compensation to workers affected by RECLAIM

There are numerous precedents for providing compensation for those negatively affected by changes in government policy. For example, when Congress planned to expand California's Redwood National Park, the loggers who would lose their jobs as a result of decreased timber production constituted a vocal and highly identifiable group who would lose. To gain their support, Congress included a provision that offered the loggers an average of $6,000 per week during the early part of the programme. Non-environmental examples of compensation to workers include the Trade Adjustment Assistance Act, which provides supplements to regular unemployment compensation when joblessness results from lower trade barriers. (This programme has been extended to workers hurt from import competition even if no trade barriers had existed.) Other examples include tax breaks to those affected by trucking deregulation and job training help to those affected by deregulation of the airlines.

These programmes suffer from several drawbacks, however. Although it may be possible to identify loggers affected by a ban on logging, it is far more difficult to determine the role that RECLAIM might play in plant closures or production declines. Firms are continually changing their production and opening and closing facilities. Determining that cost changes due to RECLAIM are responsible for specific shifts would be quite difficult.

Moreover, the net impact on workers of RECLAIM also depends upon its *stimulative* effect on other industries. Expansions lead to greater demand for workers, and that demand could absorb any declines due to RECLAIM. Direct compensation programmes seem much more sensible in isolated areas where other options are scarce and where there is little labour mobility. In contrast, the South Coast Basin is a large and diverse area with well developed labour markets.

In addition, some of the compensation programmes may not actually be very effective in helping unemployed workers find new employment. In a large labour market such as the South Coast Basin, existing private and public information programmes provide a great deal of information on employment openings. Retraining programs can be useful for those in declining occupations, but empirical studies show that some provide relatively small gains. In any event, it would be important to evaluate any informational or retraining programmes to avoid receiving relatively small gains from what could be substantial expenditures.

Finally, it is not clear that those whose jobs are lost due to RECLAIM are more deserving than other unemployed workers when it comes to income support or retraining. Given relatively fixed government budgets for support and training programmes, special programmes for those affected by RECLAIM may mean smaller benefits to other unemployed workers. Providing special compensation to a particular segment of the unemployed workforce may therefore lead to conflicts and divisions among those in need, particularly in the highly integrated labour markets of the South Coast Basin.

In sum, targeted compensation programmes such as those developed for loggers in the Redwood National Park may not be the most effective and equitable way to spend government money to deal with any unemployment effects of RECLAIM in the Los Angeles Basin.

c) Target early warning programmes for plant closings due to RECLAIM

A far less expensive way of easing hardships from unemployment is to provide advance warning so that plans can be made. One of labour's criticisms about management decisions to close facilities is that workers are told so late in the process that they can neither participate in the decisions nor make adequate plans to find other employment. Management often resists advance notice requirements because of the effect it might have on morale as well as on purchasers and clients.

The United States Environmental Protection Agency currently has a general early warning programme that is supposed to alert it to potential plant closings. The SCAQMD also has a programme to provide information to workers, firms and communities about federal assistance programmes. While this programme may not add substantially to what many *large* companies provide their workers, it might well be a useful supplement to assist employees in smaller firms that typically provide few "outplacement" benefits to laid-off workers.

c) Target investment and retraining programmes for the Los Angeles basin

It would also be possible to target compensation policies on the Los Angeles Basin as a whole, rather than on the specific workers judged to be directly affected by RECLAIM. Such policies could include stimulating new businesses, relocating workers to other areas where their skills are needed, providing training and retraining programmes to give workers new or upgraded skills, increasing government spending, or even taking over private facilities and turning them into publicly-run operations.

These programmes get around the difficulty of distinguishing the precise individuals whose unemployment is tied to RECLAIM and address the equity claims of those whose unemployment cannot be traced to RECLAIM. As emphasized above, any targeting to RECLAIM-related employees would tend to include some who would have been unemployed anyway and to exclude some whose ties to the impacts of RECLAIM are more subtle and indirect.

However, programmes targeted on the Los Angeles Basin share some of the potential difficulties discussed above. Public retraining programmes would need to be evaluated carefully to see that they provide adequate skills for jobs that would actually be available to graduates.

H. Summary of the distributive impacts of RECLAIM

The following are the principal results of the case study of the emissions trading programme proposed for the Los Angeles Basin:

- emissions trading would *reduce* overall control costs by about 40 percent compared to the equivalent command-and-control regulations;

- these cost reductions would tend to work to the advantage of *lower income* households;

- *small businesses* are likely to gain substantially from emissions trading, assuming that they receive the same initial allocation as they would under the command-and-control system;

- impacts on the costs for *individual* industries (and thus the other impacts) can differ dramatically depending upon how allowances are initially allocated;

- RECLAIM will work to the advantage of the region's *workers* in the long-term, because costs are lower and output is expanded;

- the opportunity cost of allowances may, however, dominate the cost savings from trading in the short-term in *some* product markets, leading to transitional costs to businesses and workers in those industries; and

- *mitigation or compensation measures* should be evaluated carefully to ensure that they achieve intended results and do not compromise the cost-saving gains from RECLAIM or create major administrative problems.

Perhaps the major conclusion from the case study is that a careful distributive analysis is necessary to clarify what is actually at stake when economic instruments are adopted. While small businesses and employee groups are concerned they may be harmed, in fact the empirical results show that many are likely to be big winners under the emissions trading programme.

Notes

1. The author was a member of the RECLAIM Advisory Committee.

2. Portions of this Appendix draw heavily on previous reports, including Harrison (1988), Harrison and Nichols (1990c) and especially Harrison and Nichols (1992). These reports were sponsored by the California Council for Environmental and Economic Balance and, in the case of the 1992 report, the Regulatory Flexibility Group. In addition, the author is serving as a consultant to the South Coast Air Quality Management District. The author gratefully acknowledges this support as well as the usefulness of discussions and other contributions from a number of individuals in these organizations, including Scott Johnson, Patricia Leyden, Robert Lucas, Victor Weisser, and Robert Wyman. The most substantial debt is to Albert Nichols, the coauthor of the two later reports. However, the opinions and conclusions expressed in this Appendix are those of the author and do not necessarily reflect those of any of these individuals or organizations.

    The analyses in this Appendix are subject to an important caveat. They are based upon the characteristics of RECLAIM as reported in South Coast Air Quality Management District (1992) and data available at that time. The SCAQMD is continuing to analyze the impacts of the RECLAIM proposal and to modify the key features of the program. Thus, the final rules for RECLAIM that will be considered by the Governing Board of the SCAQMD may differ from those evaluated in the Appendix. In addition, changes in the empirical information on emission control costs may lead to different estimated impacts than the ones reported in this Appendix.

3. These cost reductions are similar to those obtained in South Coast Air Quality Management District (1991a).

4. A revised air quality plan was adopted in 1991 (South Coast Air Quality Management District 1991a). However, the control measures are similar between the 1989 and 1991 plans, and thus the income distributional impacts are likely to be similar as well.

5. These estimates are based upon income rather than expenditures, which as Poterba (1991) points out should provide a more accurate proxy for permanent income. Poterba finds that a carbon tax is less regressive when income is measured by expenditures. This result implies that Figure 27 might overstate the true regressivity of control costs in the Los Angeles basin.

6. The SCAQMD agrees with this argument and proposes using permitted levels for sources subject to new source review and honoring ERCs as part of the first-year allocation calculation. However, the SCAQMD proposes allowing these modifications for only three years by requiring a three-year catchup period. Moreover, the added emissions a firm

receives according to this modification cannot, however, be sold, according to the District proposal. This feature reflects the District's view of this accommodation as a "cushion" that recognizes "today's current economic slump and provides an opportunity for increases in production." The allowance emissions cap would decline to the "standard" level if the firm were to sell the excess emission reductions (South Coast Air Quality Management District 1992).

7. See Harrison and Nichols (1992) for additional details on the cost calculations and limitations of the cost data.

8. Expanding the universe of sources to include mobile sources—such as cars, trains, and buses—could be particularly useful because they are likely to be low-cost compliers. That means that including them would lower the price of allowances and reduce the overall costs of meeting air quality goals.

9. In order to make this Appendix self-contained, the discussions in this section and the next duplicate some of the analyses in the main study.

10. This example assumes that the firm is in a "local" industry such as dry cleaning in which prices and outputs are based upon local conditions. A similar graph is presented for firms operating in national or international markets in Chapter 4 of this study.

11. The SCAQMD currently requires that new sources obtain offsets equal to 20 percent more than the emissions they would add to the Basin. The SCAQMD regulations provide that small sources can obtain offsets "for free" from a Community Bank (see Harrison and Nichols 1990).

References

Ackerman, Bruce A. and Richard B. Stewart. 1988. "Reforming Environmental Law: The Democratic Case for Market Incentives." *Columbia Journal of Environmental Law* 13:171-199.

Ackerman, Bruce A. and William Hassler. 1981. *Clean Coal/Dirty Air*. New Haven: Yale University Press.

Albert, Alain 1991. "Framework for Analyzing the Redistributive Impacts of Market-Type Mechanisms." Prepared for the OECD Meeting of Senior Budget Officials. Paris: OECD, June.

Anderson, Frederick R. et al. 1977. *Environmental Improvement Through Economic Incentives*. Baltimore: The Johns Hopkins University Press for Resources for the Future. Asch, Peter and Joseph Seneca. 1979. "Some Evidence on the Distribution of Air Quality." *Land Economics*.

Baker, Paul and Stephen Smith. 1991. "Distributional Effects of Market-Based Environmental Policy Instruments in OECD Countries." Prepared for the OECD Environment Directorate. Paris: OECD, November.

Barde, Jean-Phillipe. 1991. "The Use of Economic Instruments for Environmental Protection in OECD Countries." Presented at the *International Conference on Economy and Environment in the 90s*, August 26-27.

Barrett, Scott. 1991. "Economic Analysis of International Environmental Agreements." In *Responding to Climate Change: Selected Economic Issues*. Paris: OECD.

_____. 1992. "Side Payments in a Global Warming Convention." In *Convention on Climate Change: Economic Aspects of Negotiation*. Paris: OECD.

Baumol, William J. and Wallace E. Oates. 1979. *Economics, Environmental Policy, and the Quality of Life*. Englewood Cliffs: Prentice-Hall, Inc.

_____. 1988. *The Theory of Environmental Policy*. New York: Cambridge University Press.

Bohm, Peter. 1991. "Taxation and Environment: The Case of Sweden." Presented at the *Workshop on Taxation and Environment*. Paris: OECD, April 6-7.

Brannlund, Runar and Bengt Kriström. 1991. "Assessing the Impact of Environmental Charges: A Partial General Equilibrium Model of the Forest Sector." EFI Research Paper No. 6457. Stockholm, November.

Burtraw, Dallas and Paul R. Portney. 1991. "The Role of Compensation in Implementing Market-Based Environmental Policies." Washington, D.C.: Resources for the Future, April. Canadian Council of Ministers of the Environment. 1991. *Emission Trading: A Canadian Policy Framework*. Winnipeg, Canada: CCME.

Carlin, Alan. 1992. *The United States Experience With Economic Incentives to Control Environmental Pollution*. Report No. 230-R-92-001 prepared for the U.S. Environmental Protection Agency. Washington, D.C.: Office of Policy, Planning and Evaluation, July.

Crandall, Robert W. 1983. *Controlling Industrial Pollution: The Economics and Politics of Clean Air*. Washington, D.C.: The Brookings Institution.

Dales, J.H. 1968. *Pollution, Property, and Prices*. Toronto: University of Toronto Press.

David, Elizabeth. 1980. "Cost Effective Management Options for Attaining Water Quality." Prepared for the Department of Natural Resources Bureau of Planning. Madison, WI: DNR, October.

David, Martin et al. 1977. "Marketable Effluent Permits for the Control of Phosphorous Effluent in Lake Michigan." Social Systems Research Institute Working Paper. University of Wisconsin, December.

Delbeke, Jos. 1991. "The Prospects for the Use of Economic Instruments in EC Environmental Policy." Presented at CEPS Business Policy Seminar on *Setting New Priorities in EC Environmental Legislation*. Brussels: Commission of the European Communities, April.

Denny, Kevin and Stephen Smith. 1991. "Methods for Quantitative Assessment of the Distributional Effects of Environmental Taxes." Prepared for the OECD Environment Directorate. Paris: OECD, May.

de Savornin Lohman, A.F. 1992. "Distributional Impacts of Environmental Charges." Prepared for the OECD Workshop on *Distributive Effects of Economic Instruments in Environmental Policy*. Paris: OECD, April.

DeWitt, Diane E., Hadi Dowlatabadi, and Raymond J. Kopp. 1991. "Who Bears the Burden of Energy Taxes?" Discussion Paper No. QE91-12. Washington, DC: Resources for the Future, March.

Dorfman, Nancy S. and Arthur Snow. 1975. "Who Will Pay for Pollution Control?" *National Tax Journal* 28 (March):101-115.

Downing, Paul and L. White. 1986. "Innovation in Pollution Control." *Journal of Environmental Economics and Management* 13:18-27.

Dudek, Daniel J. and John Palmisano. 1988. "Emissions Trading: Why is this Thoroughbred Hobbled?" *Columbia Journal of Environmental Law* 13(2):217-256.

Elman, Barry S., Tom Tyler, and Michael Doonan. 1992. "Economic Incentives Under the New Clean Air Act." Paper prepared for the *85th Annual Meeting of the Air and Waste Management Association.* Kansas City, MO: A&WMA, June.

Freeman, A. Myrick. 1972. "Distribution of Environmental Quality." In *Environmental Quality: Theory and Method in the Social Sciences.* A.V. Kneese and B.T. Bowers (Eds.). Baltimore, MD: Johns Hopkins University Press for Resources for the Future.Gianessi, Leonard P., Henry M. Peskin, and Edward Wolff. 1979. "The Distributional Effects of Uniform Air Pollution Policy in the United States." *The Quarterly Journal of Economics* 93(2):281-31

Goldfarb, Robert S. 1980. "Compensating the Victims of Policy Change." *Regulation* 4(5):22-30.

Hahn, Robert W. and Roger G. Noll. 1982. "Designing a Market for Tradable Emission Permits." In *Reform of Environmental Regulation.* Wesley A. Magat (Ed.). Cambridge, MA: Ballinger Publishing Company.

Hahn, Robert W. and Gordon L. Hester. 1989. "Marketable Permits: Lessons for Theory and Practice." *Ecology Law Quarterly* 16(2):361-406.

Harrison, David, Jr. 1974. *Who Pays for Clean Air?* Cambridge, MA: Ballinger Publishing Company.

____. 1981. "Regulation and Distribution: An Agenda for Research." In *Creating an Agenda for Regulatory Research*, A. Ferguson (Ed.). Cambridge, MA: Ballinger Publishing Company.

_____. 1983. "The Problem of Aircraft Noise." In *Incentives for Environmental Protection.* Thomas C. Schelling (Ed.). Cambridge, MA: MIT Press.

_____. 1988. *Economic Impacts of the Draft Air Quality Management Plan Proposed by the South Coast Air Quality Management District.* Prepared for the California Council for Environmental and Economic Balance. Cambridge, MA: National Economic Research Associates, Inc., December.

_____. 1989. *Policy Approaches to Controlling Greenhouse Gases.* Cambridge, MA: National Economic Research Associates, Inc., May.

Harrison, David, Jr. and Daniel L. Rubinfeld. 1978a. "Hedonic Housing Values and the Demand for Clean Air." *Journal of Environmental Economics and Management* 5(March).

_____. 1978b. "The Distribution of Benefits from Improvements in Urban Air Quality." *Journal of Environmental Economics and Management* 5:313-332.

Harrison, David, Jr. and Paul R. Portney. 1982. "Who Loses from Reform of Environmental Regulation." In *Reform of Environmental Regulation*. Wesley A. Magat (Ed.). Cambridge, MA: Ballinger Publishing Company.

Harrison, David, Jr. and Albert L. Nichols. 1990a. *Benefits of the 1989 Air Quality Management Plan for the South Coast Air Basin: A Reassessment*. Prepared for the California Council for Environmental and Economic Balance. Cambridge, MA: National Economic Research Associates, Inc., March.

_____. 1990b. "Market-Based Approaches for Environmental Protection: Implications for Business." In *Special Report on Global Environmental Issues*. Bradford Gentry (Ed.). Washington, D.C.: The Bureau of National Affairs.

_____. 1990c. *Market-Based Approaches to Reduce the Cost of Clean Air in California's South Coast Basin*. Prepared for the California Council for Environmental and Economic Balance, Cambridge, MA: National Economic Research Associates, Inc., November.

_____. 1992. *An Economic Analysis of the RECLAIM Trading Programme for the South Coast Air Basin*. Prepared for the Regulatory Flexibility Group and the California Council for Environmental and Economic Balance. Cambridge, MA: National Economic Research Associates, Inc., March.

Harrison, David, Jr., Albert L. Nichols, John S. Evans, and J. Douglas Zona. 1992. *Valuation of Air Pollution Damages*. Prepared for Southern California Edison Company. Cambridge, MA: National Economic Research Associates, Inc., March.

Hoeller, Peter, Andrew Dean, and Jon Nicolaisen. 1991. "Macroeconomic Implications of Reducing Greenhouse Gas Emissions: A Survey of Empirical Studies." *OECD Economic Studies* 16:3-36.

Howarth, David, Paul Nikitopoulus and Gary Yohe. 1990. "On the Ability of Carbon Taxes to Fend Off Greenhouse Warming." *OPEC Review* Spring.

ICF Resources, Inc. 1989. *Economic, Environmental, and Coal Market Impacts of SO_2 Emissions Trading Under Alternative Acid Rain Control Proposals*. Prepared for the U.S. Environmental Protection Agency Office of Policy, Planning and Evaluation and the U.S. Department of the Interior Office of Program Analysis. Washington, DC: ICF Resources, Inc., March.

Industrial Gas Cleaning Institute, Inc. 1990. "Acid Rain Controls Would Create Thousands of Jobs, Analyses Find." Press Release. Washington, DC: IGCI, March.

Johnson, Paul, Steve McKay, and Stephen Smith. 1990. "The Distributional Consequences of Environmental Taxes." Commentary Number 23. London: The Institute for Fiscal Studies, July.

Kete, Nancy. 1992. "The U.S. Acid Rain Control Allowance Trading System." In *Climate Change: Designing a Tradeable Permit System*. Paris: OECD

Kneese, Allen V. and Charles L. Schultze. 1976. *Pollution, Prices and Public Policy*. Washington, D.C.: The Brookings Institution.

Lambert, Peter J. 1989. *The Distribution and Redistribution of Income: A Mathematical Analysis*. Cambridge, MA: Basil Blackwell, Inc.

Leone, Robert A. 1986. *Who Profits: Winners, Losers, and Government Regulation*. New York: Basic Books, Inc. Publishers.

Leone, Robert A. and John E. Jackson. 1981. "The Political Economy of Federal Regulatory Activity." In *Studies in Public Regulation*, G. Fromm (Ed.). Cambridge: MIT Press.

Magat, Wesley A., Alan J. Krupnick, and Winston Harrington. 1986. *Rules in the Making: A Statistical Analysis of Regulatory Agency Behavior*. Washington, D.C.: Resources for the Future.

McKay, Steve, Mark Pearson, and Stephen Smith. 1990. "Fiscal Instruments in Environmental Policy." *Fiscal Studies* 11(4):1-20.

Milliman, S. and R. Prince. 1989. "Firm Incentives to Promote Technological Change in Pollution Control." *Journal of Environmental Economics and Management* 17:247-265.

Musgrave, Richard A. and Peggy B. Musgrave. 1984. *Public Finance in Theory and Practice*. New York: McGraw-Hill Book Company.

Nichols, Albert L. 1983. "The Regulation of Airborne Benzene." In *Incentives for Environmental Protection*, Thomas C. Schelling (Ed.). Cambridge, MA: MIT Press, 145-219.

_____. 1984. *Targeting Economic Incentives for Environmental Protection*. Cambridge, MA: MIT Press.

_____. 1992. *Emissions Trading Program for Stationary Sources of NO_x in Ontario (Draft)*. Prepared for Advisory Group on Emission Trading with assistance from Goodfellow Consultants, Inc. and VHB Research and Consulting, Inc. Cambridge, MA: National Economic Research Associates, Inc., August.

Nichols, Albert L. and David Harrison, Jr. 1990a. *Using Emissions Trading to Reduce Ground-Level Ozone in Canada: A Feasibility Analysis*. Prepared for Environment Canada. Cambridge, MA: National Economic Research Associates, Inc., November.

_____. 1990b. *The Impact on Ontario Hydro of Emissions Trading for Nitrogen Oxides: A Preliminary Analysis*. Prepared for Ontario Hydro. Cambridge, MA: National Economic Research Associates, Inc., December.

_____. 1991. *Market-Based Approaches to Managing Air Emissions in Alberta.* Prepared for Alberta Energy, Alberta Environment, and the Canadian Petroleum Association. Cambridge, MA: National Economic Research Associates, Inc., February.

Noll, Roger G. 1990. "Marketable Emissions Permits in Los Angeles." Stanford, CA: Stanford University Department of Economics, December.

Organisation for Economic Co-Operation and Development. 1989. *Economic Instruments for Environmental Protection.* Paris: OECD.

_____. 1991a. "Recommendation of the Council on the Use of Economic Instruments in Environmental Policy." Paris: OECD, January.

_____. 1991b. "Guidelines for the Application of Economic Instruments in Environmental Policy." Background Paper Number 1. Paris: Environment Committee Meeting at Ministerial Level, January.

_____. 1991c. *Environmental Policy: How to Apply Economic Instruments.* Paris: OECD.

_____. 1991d. "The Use of Economic Instruments for Environmental Protection in OECD Countries: An Assessment." Presented at the *Ad Hoc Meeting on Economic Instruments for Environmental Policies for Countries in Transition.* Geneva, Switzerland: OECD, December.

_____. 1992a. "The Costs of Reducing CO_2 Emissions: Evidence from Green." Paris: Working Party 1 of the Economic Policy Committee, March.

_____. 1992b. *Climate Change: Designing a Tradeable Permit System.* Paris: OECD.Osten, James A., George Vasic, and David West. 1991. "Carbon Dioxide Emissions and Federal Energy Policy: A Discussion of the Economic Consequences of Alternative Taxes." Prepared for Imperial Oil, Ltd. Washington, DC: DRI/McGraw-Hill, March.

Palmer, Adele R. et al. 1980. *Economic Implications of Regulating Chlorofluorocarbon Emissions from Nonaerosol Applications.* Report Number R-2524-EPA. Santa Monica, CA: Rand Corporation, June.

Palmer, Adele R. and Timothy H. Quinn. 1980. *Allocating Chlorofluorocarbon Permits: Who Gains, Who Loses, and What is the Cost?* Report Number R-2806-EPA. Santa Monica: Rand Corporation, July.

Pearce, David. 1991. "The Role of Carbon Taxes in Adjusting to Global Warming." *The Economic Journal* 101(July):938-948.

Pearce, David, Anel Markandya, and Edward Barbier. 1989. *Sustainable Development: The Implications of Sustainable Development for Resource Accounting, Project Appraisal and Integrative Environmental Policy.* London: London Environmental Economics Centre.

Pearson, Mark and Stephen Smith. 1991. *The European Carbon Tax: An Assessment of the European Commission's Proposals*. London: The Institute for Fiscal Studies, December.

Peskin, Henry M. 1978. "Environmental Policy and the Distribution of Benefits and Costs." In *Current Issues in U.S. Environmental Policy*, Paul R. Portney (Ed.). Baltimore, MD: Johns Hopkins University Press for Resources for the Future.

Portney, Paul R. (Editor). 1990. *Public Policies for Environmental Protection*. Washington, D.C.: Resources for the Future.

Poterba, James M. 1991. "Tax Policy to Combat Global Warming: On Designing a Carbon Tax." In R. Dornbusch and J.M. Poterba (Eds.), *Global Warming: Economic Policy Responses*. Cambridge, MA: MIT Press.

Repetto, Robert, Roger C. Dower, Robin Jenkins, and Jacqueline Geoghegan. 1992. *Green Fees: How a Tax Shift Can Work for the Environment and the Economy*. Washington, D.C.: World Resources Institute, November.

Robison, H. David. 1985. "Who Pays for Industrial Pollution Abatement?" *Review of Economics and Statistics* LXVII(November):702-706.

Schelling, Thomas C. (Editor). 1983. *Incentives for Environmental Protection*. Cambridge, MA: MIT Press.

Schillo, Bruce et al. 1992. "The Distributional Impacts of a Carbon Tax." Washington, DC: U.S. Environmental Protection Agency, Energy Policy Branch, February.

Schultze, Charles L. 1977. *The Public Use of Private Interest*. Washington, D.C.: Brookings Institution.

Schmalensee, Richard. 1990. *United States Experience with the Emissions Trading Approach*. Washington, D.C.: Department of State.

Schwartz, Joel. 1992. "Marketable Permits: The NO_x Universe." Recommendations of the Coalition for Clean Air. Venice, CA: Coalition for Clean Air, January.

Scott, Sue. 1991. "Carbon Taxes: Theoretical Considerations and Estimates of the Effects on Households." Presented to The Economic and Social Research Institute Conference on *Controlling Carbon Dioxide Emissions: The Economic Implications for Ireland*. Dublin: ESRI, November.

Shackleton, Robert et al. 1992. "The Efficiency Value of Carbon Tax Revenues." Draft paper prepared for the Stanford Energy Modeling Forum 12. Washington, DC: U.S. Environmental Protection Agency, Energy Policy Branch, March.

Shah, Anwar and Bjorn Larsen. 1992. "Carbon Taxes, the Greenhouse Effect, and Developing Countries." Background Paper No. 6 for the *World Development Report 1992*. Washington, DC: The World Bank, March.

South Coast Air Quality Management District. 1991a. *Air Quality Assessment and Socio-Economic Impacts - "Implementation: Implications for the Basin."* Marketable Permits Program Working Paper No. 5. Los Angeles, CA: South Coast Air Quality Management District, December.

_____. 1991b. *Draft Final 1991 Air Quality Management Plan, South Coast Air Basin.* Los Angeles, CA: South Coast Air Quality Management District and Southern California Association of Governments, May.

_____. 1992. *RECLAIM: Marketable Permits Program Summary Recommendations.* Los Angeles, CA: South Coast Air Quality Management District, Spring.

Stavins, Robert N. 1988. *Project 88: Harnessing Market Forces to protect the Environment: Initiatives for the New President.* Washington, D.C.: Senators Heinz and Wirth.

_____. 1991. *Project 88 Round II -- Incentives for Action: Designing Market-Based Environmental Strategies.* Washington, D.C.: Senators Heinz and Wirth.

Stavins, Robert N. and Bradley W. Whitehead. 1992. *The Greening of America's Taxes: Pollution Charges and Environmental Protection.* Washington, DC: Progressive Policy Institute, February.

Stewart, Richard B. 1990. *A "Comprehensive" Approach to Addressing Potential Global Climate Change.* Washington, D.C.: Department of State.

Task Force on the Environment and the Internal Market. 1989. *1992: The Environmental Dimension.* Brussels: Commission of the European Communities.

Terkla, David. 1984. "The Efficiency Value of Effluent Tax Revenues." *Journal of Environmental Economics and Management.*

Tietenberg, Thomas H. 1985. *Emissions Trading, An Exercise in Reforming Pollution Policy.* Washington, D.C.: Resources for the Future.

_____. 1992. "Relevant Experience with Tradeable Entitlements." In *Combating Global Warming: Study on a Global System of Tradeable Carbon Emission Entitlements.* New York, NY: United Nations.

U.S. Congress. 1990. *Carbon Charges as a Response to Global Warming: The Effects of Taxing Fossil Fuels.* Washington, DC: Congressional Budget Office, August.

United Nations Conference on Trade and Development 1992. *Combating Global Warming: Study on a Global System of Tradeable Carbon Emission Entitlements.* New York, NY: United Nations.

Weitzman, Martin. 1974. "Prices vs. Quantities." *Review of Economic Studies* 41 (October):477-491.

Whalley, John and Randall Wigle. 1990. "The International Incidence of Carbon Taxes." Presented at the Istituto Bancario Sao Paolo di Torino Conference on *Economic Policy Responses to Global Warming*, Palazzo Colonna, Rome, October.

White, Lawrence J. 1982. *The Regulation of Air Pollutant Emissions from Motor Vehicles.* Washington, D.C.: American Enterprise Institute.

Wile, John H. 1991. "Impacts of the 1990 Clean Air Act on Utility Planning." *The Electricity Journal* 4(7):46-53, August/September.

Wyman, Robert. 1991. *A Marketable Permits Program for the South Coast: Comments of the Regulatory Flexibility Group.* Los Angeles, CA: Regulatory Flexibility Group, December.

Zupan, Jeffrey M. 1973. *The Distribution of Air Quality in the New York Region.* Washington, DC: Resources for the Future, Inc.

MAIN SALES OUTLETS OF OECD PUBLICATIONS
PRINCIPAUX POINTS DE VENTE DES PUBLICATIONS DE L'OCDE

ARGENTINA – ARGENTINE
Carlos Hirsch S.R.L.
Galería Güemes, Florida 165, 4° Piso
1333 Buenos Aires   Tel. (1) 331.1787 y 331.2391
                               Telefax: (1) 331.1787

AUSTRALIA – AUSTRALIE
D.A. Information Services
648 Whitehorse Road, P.O.B 163
Mitcham, Victoria 3132   Tel. (03) 873.4411
                               Telefax: (03) 873.5679

AUSTRIA – AUTRICHE
Gerold & Co.
Graben 31
Wien I   Tel. (0222) 533.50.14

BELGIUM – BELGIQUE
Jean De Lannoy
Avenue du Roi 202
B-1060 Bruxelles   Tel. (02) 538.51.69/538.08.41
                               Telefax: (02) 538.08.41

CANADA
Renouf Publishing Company Ltd.
1294 Algoma Road
Ottawa, ON K1B 3W8   Tel. (613) 741.4333
                               Telefax: (613) 741.5439
Stores:
61 Sparks Street
Ottawa, ON K1P 5R1   Tel. (613) 238.8985
211 Yonge Street
Toronto, ON M5B 1M4   Tel. (416) 363.3171
                               Telefax: (416)363.59.63
Les Éditions La Liberté Inc.
3020 Chemin Sainte-Foy
Sainte-Foy, PQ G1X 3V6   Tel. (418) 658.3763
                               Telefax: (418) 658.3763

Federal Publications Inc.
165 University Avenue, Suite 701
Toronto, ON M5H 3B8   Tel. (416) 860.1611
                               Telefax: (416) 860.1608
Les Publications Fédérales
1185 Université
Montréal, QC H3B 3A7   Tel. (514) 954.1633
                               Telefax : (514) 954.1635

CHINA – CHINE
China National Publications Import
Export Corporation (CNPIEC)
16 Gongti E. Road, Chaoyang District
P.O. Box 88 or 50
Beijing 100704 PR   Tel. (01) 506.6688
                               Telefax: (01) 506.3101

DENMARK – DANEMARK
Munksgaard Book and Subscription Service
35, Nørre Søgade, P.O. Box 2148
DK-1016 København K   Tel. (33) 12.85.70
                               Telefax: (33) 12.93.87

FINLAND – FINLANDE
Akateeminen Kirjakauppa
Keskuskatu 1, P.O. Box 128
00100 Helsinki
Subscription Services/Agence d'abonnements :
P.O. Box 23
00371 Helsinki   Tel. (358 0) 12141
                               Telefax: (358 0) 121.4450

FRANCE
OECD/OCDE
Mail Orders/Commandes par correspondance:
2, rue André-Pascal
75775 Paris Cedex 16   Tel. (33-1) 45.24.82.00
Telefax: (33-1) 45.24.81.76   or (33-1) 45.24.85.00
                               Telex: 640048 OCDE

OECD Bookshop/Librairie de l'OCDE :
33, rue Octave-Feuillet
75016 Paris   Tel. (33-1) 45.24.81.67
                               (33-1) 45.24.81.81
Documentation Française
29, quai Voltaire
75007 Paris   Tel. 40.15.70.00
Gibert Jeune (Droit-Économie)
6, place Saint-Michel
75006 Paris   Tel. 43.25.91.19
Librairie du Commerce International
10, avenue d'Iéna
75016 Paris   Tel. 40.73.34.60
Librairie Dunod
Université Paris-Dauphine
Place du Maréchal de Lattre de Tassigny
75016 Paris   Tel. (1) 44.05.40.13
Librairie Lavoisier
11, rue Lavoisier
75008 Paris   Tel. 42.65.39.95
Librairie L.G.D.J. - Montchrestien
20, rue Soufflot
75005 Paris   Tel. 46.33.89.85
Librairie des Sciences Politiques
30, rue Saint-Guillaume
75007 Paris   Tel. 45.48.36.02
P.U.F.
49, boulevard Saint-Michel
75005 Paris   Tel. 43.25.83.40
Librairie de l'Université
12a, rue Nazareth
13100 Aix-en-Provence   Tel. (16) 42.26.18.08
Documentation Française
165, rue Garibaldi
69003 Lyon   Tel. (16) 78.63.32.23
Librairie Decitre
29, place Bellecour
69002 Lyon   Tel. (16) 72.40.54.54

GERMANY – ALLEMAGNE
OECD Publications and Information Centre
August-Bebel-Allee 6
D-53175 Bonn 2   Tel. (0228) 959.120
                               Telefax: (0228) 959.12.17

GREECE – GRÈCE
Librairie Kauffmann
Mavrokordatou 9
106 78 Athens   Tel. (01) 32.55.321
                               Telefax: (01) 36.33.967

HONG-KONG
Swindon Book Co. Ltd.
13–15 Lock Road
Kowloon, Hong Kong   Tel. 366.80.31
                               Telefax: 739.49.75

HUNGARY – HONGRIE
Euro Info Service
POB 1271
1464 Budapest   Tel. (1) 111.62.16
                               Telefax : (1) 111.60.61

ICELAND – ISLANDE
Mál Mog Menning
Laugavegi 18, Pósthólf 392
121 Reykjavik   Tel. 162.35.23

INDIA – INDE
Oxford Book and Stationery Co.
Scindia House
New Delhi 110001   Tel.(11) 331.5896/5308
                               Telefax: (11) 332.5993
17 Park Street
Calcutta 700016   Tel. 240832

INDONESIA – INDONÉSIE
Pdii-Lipi
P.O. Box 269/JKSMG/88
Jakarta 12790   Tel. 583467
                               Telex: 62 875

IRELAND – IRLANDE
TDC Publishers – Library Suppliers
12 North Frederick Street
Dublin 1   Tel. (01) 874.48.35
                               Telefax: (01) 874.84.16

ISRAEL
Electronic Publications only
Publications électroniques seulement
Sophist Systems Ltd.
71 Allenby Street
Tel-Aviv 65134   Tel. 3-29.00.21
                               Telefax: 3-29.92.39

ITALY – ITALIE
Libreria Commissionaria Sansoni
Via Duca di Calabria 1/1
50125 Firenze   Tel. (055) 64.54.15
                               Telefax: (055) 64.12.57
Via Bartolini 29
20155 Milano   Tel. (02) 36.50.83
Editrice e Libreria Herder
Piazza Montecitorio 120
00186 Roma   Tel. 679.46.28
                               Telefax: 678.47.51
Libreria Hoepli
Via Hoepli 5
20121 Milano   Tel. (02) 86.54.46
                               Telefax: (02) 805.28.86
Libreria Scientifica
Dott. Lucio de Biasio 'Aeiou'
Via Coronelli, 6
20146 Milano   Tel. (02) 48.95.45.52
                               Telefax: (02) 48.95.45.48

JAPAN – JAPON
OECD Publications and Information Centre
Landic Akasaka Building
2-3-4 Akasaka, Minato-ku
Tokyo 107   Tel. (81.3) 3586.2016
                               Telefax: (81.3) 3584.7929

KOREA – CORÉE
Kyobo Book Centre Co. Ltd.
P.O. Box 1658, Kwang Hwa Moon
Seoul   Tel. 730.78.91
                               Telefax: 735.00.30

MALAYSIA – MALAISIE
Co-operative Bookshop Ltd.
University of Malaya
P.O. Box 1127, Jalan Pantai Baru
59700 Kuala Lumpur
Malaysia   Tel. 756.5000/756.5425
                               Telefax: 757.3661

MEXICO – MEXIQUE
Revistas y Periodicos Internacionales S.A. de C.V.
Florencia 57 - 1004
Mexico, D.F. 06600   Tel. 207.81.00
                               Telefax : 208.39.79

NETHERLANDS – PAYS-BAS
SDU Uitgeverij Plantijnstraat
Externe Fondsen
Postbus 20014
2500 EA's-Gravenhage   Tel. (070) 37.89.880
Voor bestellingen: Telefax: (070) 34.75.778

**NEW ZEALAND
NOUVELLE-ZÉLANDE**
Legislation Services
P.O. Box 12418
Thorndon, Wellington   Tel. (04) 496.5652
                              Telefax: (04) 496.5698

NORWAY – NORVÈGE
Narvesen Info Center – NIC
Bertrand Narvesens vei 2
P.O. Box 6125 Etterstad
0602 Oslo 6   Tel. (022) 57.33.00
                              Telefax: (022) 68.19.01

PAKISTAN
Mirza Book Agency
65 Shahrah Quaid-E-Azam
Lahore 54000   Tel. (42) 353.601
                              Telefax: (42) 231.730

PHILIPPINE – PHILIPPINES
International Book Center
5th Floor, Filipinas Life Bldg.
Ayala Avenue
Metro Manila   Tel. 81.96.76
                              Telex 23312 RHP PH

PORTUGAL
Livraria Portugal
Rua do Carmo 70-74
Apart. 2681
1200 Lisboa   Tel.: (01) 347.49.82/5
                              Telefax: (01) 347.02.64

SINGAPORE – SINGAPOUR
Information Publications Pte. Ltd.
41, Kallang Pudding, No. 04-03
Singapore 1334   Tel. 741.5166
                              Telefax: 742.9356

SPAIN – ESPAGNE
Mundi-Prensa Libros S.A.
Castelló 37, Apartado 1223
Madrid 28001   Tel. (91) 431.33.99
                              Telefax: (91) 575.39.98

Libreria Internacional AEDOS
Consejo de Ciento 391
08009 – Barcelona   Tel. (93) 488.30.09
                              Telefax: (93) 487.76.59

Llibreria de la Generalitat
Palau Moja
Rambla dels Estudis, 118
08002 – Barcelona
            (Subscripcions) Tel. (93) 318.80.12
            (Publicacions) Tel. (93) 302.67.23
                              Telefax: (93) 412.18.54

SRI LANKA
Centre for Policy Research
c/o Colombo Agencies Ltd.
No. 300-304, Galle Road
Colombo 3   Tel. (1) 574240, 573551-2
                              Telefax: (1) 575394, 510711

SWEDEN – SUÈDE
Fritzes Information Center
Box 16356
Regeringsgatan 12
106 47 Stockholm   Tel. (08) 690.90.90
                              Telefax: (08) 20.50.21

Subscription Agency/Agence d'abonnements :
Wennergren-Williams Info AB
P.O. Box 1305
171 25 Solna   Tel. (08) 705.97.50
                              Téléfax : (08) 27.00.71

SWITZERLAND – SUISSE
Maditec S.A. (Books and Periodicals - Livres
et périodiques)
Chemin des Palettes 4
Case postale 266
1020 Renens   Tel. (021) 635.08.65
                              Telefax: (021) 635.07.80

Librairie Payot S.A.
4, place Pépinet
CP 3212
1002 Lausanne   Tel. (021) 341.33.48
                              Telefax: (021) 341.33.45

Librairie Unilivres
6, rue de Candolle
1205 Genève   Tel. (022) 320.26.23
                              Telefax: (022) 329.73.18

Subscription Agency/Agence d'abonnements :
Dynapresse Marketing S.A.
38 avenue Vibert
1227 Carouge   Tel.: (022) 308.07.89
                              Telefax : (022) 308.07.99

See also – Voir aussi :
OECD Publications and Information Centre
August-Bebel-Allee 6
D-53175 Bonn 2 (Germany)   Tel. (0228) 959.120
                              Telefax: (0228) 959.12.17

TAIWAN – FORMOSE
Good Faith Worldwide Int'l. Co. Ltd.
9th Floor, No. 118, Sec. 2
Chung Hsiao E. Road
Taipei   Tel. (02) 391.7396/391.7397
                              Telefax: (02) 394.9176

THAILAND – THAÏLANDE
Suksit Siam Co. Ltd.
113, 115 Fuang Nakhon Rd.
Opp. Wat Rajbopith
Bangkok 10200   Tel. (662) 225.9531/2
                              Telefax: (662) 222.5188

TURKEY – TURQUIE
Kültür Yayinlari Is-Türk Ltd. Sti.
Atatürk Bulvari No. 191/Kat 13
Kavaklidere/Ankara   Tel. 428.11.40 Ext. 2458
Dolmabahce Cad. No. 29
Besiktas/Istanbul   Tel. 260.71.88
                              Telex: 43482B

UNITED KINGDOM – ROYAUME-UNI
HMSO
Gen. enquiries   Tel. (071) 873 0011
Postal orders only:
P.O. Box 276, London SW8 5DT
Personal Callers HMSO Bookshop
49 High Holborn, London WC1V 6HB
                              Telefax: (071) 873 8200
Branches at: Belfast, Birmingham, Bristol, Edin-
burgh, Manchester

UNITED STATES – ÉTATS-UNIS
OECD Publications and Information Centre
2001 L Street N.W., Suite 700
Washington, D.C. 20036-4910 Tel. (202) 785.6323
                              Telefax: (202) 785.0350

VENEZUELA
Libreria del Este
Avda F. Miranda 52, Aptdo. 60337
Edificio Galipán
Caracas 106   Tel. 951.1705/951.2307/951.1297
                              Telegram: Libreste Caracas

Subscription to OECD periodicals may also be
placed through main subscription agencies.

Les abonnements aux publications périodiques de
l'OCDE peuvent être souscrits auprès des
principales agences d'abonnement.

Orders and inquiries from countries where Distribu-
tors have not yet been appointed should be sent to:
OECD Publications Service, 2 rue André-Pascal,
75775 Paris Cedex 16, France.

Les commandes provenant de pays où l'OCDE n'a
pas encore désigné de distributeur devraient être
adressées à : OCDE, Service des Publications,
2, rue André-Pascal, 75775 Paris Cedex 16, France.

12-1993

OECD PUBLICATIONS, 2 rue André-Pascal, 75775 PARIS CEDEX 16
PRINTED IN FRANCE
(97 94 03 3) ISBN 92-64-04026-9 - No. 47019 1994